SHRINKIN' STINKIN' THINKIN'
A Guide To Raising Self-Esteem In Children

Copyright © 2003 by MaryAnn Brittingham

Printed in the United States of America

Published by: Buster B. B. Publishing
1530 Indian Springs Road
Pine Bush, NY 12566
Phone: 845-744-3213

Edited by: Amy Short, Ann Corrao and Marlena Lange

Illustrated by: Mike Corrao Jr.

Book design by: John D. Yozzo

Cover design by: Lisa Beattie

ISBN   0-9726691-0-8

Library of Congress Control Number 2002096805

D1563021

☺

This book is dedicated
with my deepest love and appreciation

To my husband George,
Who has supported and encouraged all my endeavors,
Who has brought great joy into my life,
Thank you for your love, humor
and unwavering belief in me.

To Mom and Dad,
For your unconditional love and faith in me.

Mary Ann Brittengham

Acknowledgements

This book has been a true labor of love for me and a dream come true. I could never have done it alone. Many special people guided, supported and encouraged me through this process, and I would like to express heartfelt appreciation and gratitude for their contributions.

My siblings, their spouses and their children who have all in their own special ways contributed to this book. A special thanks to my sister Phyllis, who I could always count on for love, support and honesty. You are the kind of sister and friend everyone needs. Thank you for encouraging me to turn my dream into a reality.

Amy Berger Short – Thank you for your patience in making sense out of my non-sense while editing the first draft, without your careful and professional critique at the early stages, I could not have taken the next step.

Ann Corrao – Thank you for freely giving so much of your time to help me turn this into a book. You gave me invaluable help with the style, flow, reorganizing and rewriting. You have been everything an author needs: A gentle critic and editor, a trusted advisor, an understanding listener and a great source of encouragement. Over the years, your love, wisdom and strength have inspired me to be the best I can be. Thanks Mom!

Gordon Corrao – Thank you for reading each draft and for being there with either good advice or a good laugh. Your endless encouragement and insightful remarks help to keep me focused on what is really important in life. You model generosity and kindness on a daily basis. You have helped me to keep things in perspective, taught me not to sweat the small stuff and when all else fails, use Duct Tape!!! Who would have thought my youngest brother could teach me so much.

Michael Corrao, Jr. – Thank you for your willingness to work under time restraints. You are truly a creative and gifted artist. I really enjoyed working with you and look forward to future endeavors together.

Marlena Lange – Thank you for generously taking time out of your busy schedule to edit the book. Your positive outlook, kindness and gentle ways reflect many of the teachings I emphasize not only here but in my workshops.

Holly Jeffery and Bobbie Howard – Over the years you have been more than generous with your time, resources, creative ideas and professional skills in helping me develop my business. I appreciate all your guidance and most of all the laughter we've shared.

John D. Yozzo (aka: TopWop) – You are such a generous and giving man. Without a moments hesitation you offered to help me with this huge endeavor. I'm sure you never realized just how much time you would have to give up at the golf course, yet you never once complained (at least not to me). Your patience with all my changes and indecision was above and beyond the call of duty!!! What a blessing it is to have an uncle with so much knowledge and so many resources at his fingertips. Thank you for your guidance and all the humorous e-mails that kept me laughing when I wanted to cry.

My husband George – You originally encouraged (nagged) me to write this book never realizing how many nights you would spend alone eating microwave meals. ☺ Thank you for proofreading and for being there to encourage me through every phase of this book. Thank you for filling my days with love and laughter.

Foreword

I hope a lot of people buy this book so my niece can get her nose job and a bunch of others, who I don't even know, can get a lot of self-esteem.

I've known MaryAnn her entire life, although I wasn't there when she was born because I had my own apartment . . . or I might have been overseas . . . I'm not sure. Doesn't matter, anyway. I'm still her uncle.

MaryAnn had low self-esteem when she was growing up only because there wasn't enough to go around. Having seven brothers and sisters with whom to compete, self-esteem was at a premium. It was only available on alternate Thursdays during the summer and every other weekend the rest of the year. But MaryAnn was tough. She scratched and clawed her way to the top and ended up with **ALL** the self-esteem. Not knowing what to do with the self-esteem she didn't need, and not wanting to waste it, she decided to write this book and share her wealth.

I got involved because I'm basically stupid. I recall asking myself what I could do to completely disrupt my life - - which up until then consisted of playing golf and lying about my score. The answer came back, a couple of days later while I was putting: "Call MaryAnn. She'll let you do the graphics on her book." I thought I had enough self-esteem to resist but when I checked I found out she had it ALL. I wanted some. I did the book.

Actually, this is a darn good book. My niece is brilliant. Everything she espouses is that which I have followed throughout my life. It has worked with my daughter, my granddaughters, and everyone else to whom I have imparted the knowledge.

Read. Learn. Practice. Everyone's self-esteem will soar.

Uncle John D. Yozzo (aka: TopWop)

Table of Contents

THE BEGINNING

THERE IS NO SUCH THING AS A PERFECT PARENT.

Parenting is one of the most difficult and frustrating jobs in the world. Before you became a parent you may have thought you were going to be the most patient, the most accepting and the most nurturing parent. Then reality set in. You had children that were active and imperfect. Wouldn't it be ideal to have the patience of Job, the dedication of June Clever and the sense of humor of Cliff Huxtable? Where is that script anyhow? Help! I need it.

I can hear some of you saying, "I know I could be a more perfect parent if I had eight hours sleep each night, if the laundry was done, if there was more money in the bank than bills on the desk, if work always went well and relationships at home were totally loving and respectful, if I didn't have so much stress, what a great parent I would be!" Stress in your life has a tremendous impact on how you interact with your children. Your children often get the brunt of your anger from stress because it is easier to take it out on them than on your boss or spouse.

Most of us follow the patterns of learned behavior from our upbringing. Your parents didn't have parenting classes and so you learned by watching their behaviors. You may have promised as we all do, "I will never say and do the mean things my parents said or did to me." However in heated and stressful moment you go on "automatic pilot" and your parents' words just gush out of your mouth. It takes practice and time to reprogram those "old tapes." We are given little or no training on how to raise confident, productive children. Just because you were a child once does not mean you know how to raise one.

It needs to be said that no one is blaming the parents. Parents don't realize that some forms of negative management would have the opposite effect of what they really want. I believe most parents do the best they can but most simply fly by the seat of their pants. The fact is you, and your children, have to live with the results of your unintentional mistakes. And these mistakes have a way of being passed on to future generations. I am looking to break the negative pattern of the past so that your children can have a more hopeful future.

WARNING: I will be viewing some of the behaviors parents display that may affect a child's self-esteem in negative ways. I do not do this so you can beat yourselves up (you probably already do enough of that). I discuss it because I believe in order to change a behavior you first have to recognize that the behavior exists. Please also note that if you do exhibit any or all of the behaviors I discuss, you have not ruined your child for life. Keep in mind:

- It is the frequency and intensity in which it is done.

- All things can turn positive if you are willing to change the negative behaviors.

BE AWARE:

Everything suggested in this book is easier said than done.

You can probably rattle off hundreds of suggestions to friends or neighbors on how they can help their children, but when it comes to your own, it is a greater challenge to put those suggestions into action. When it is your own child, you tend to personalize the behavior more and lose patience with yourself and your child.

No one says parenting is easy. I do not want you to think that accepting and using the behaviors suggested will turn your child around overnight. Wouldn't it be wonderful if you could flex your arm a few times and build a bulging muscle? Or push away from the table once or twice and lose 10 pounds? Just as this is a fantasy, doing any of the skills in this book once or twice will not build you or your child's self-esteem. You will need to practice, have patience, and be persistent until it becomes second nature to you. It takes time.

Keep in mind it is never too late to start and it is never too late to change!

You will never "Have it all together.
That's like trying to eat once and for all"

Twelve Rules for Raising Delinquent Children

1. Begin with infancy to give the child everything he wants. In this way, he will grow up to believe the world owes him a living.

2. When he picks up bad words, laugh at him. This will make him think he's cute.

3. Never give him any spiritual training. Wait until he is twenty-one and then let him "decide for himself."

4. Avoid use of the word "wrong". It may develop a guilt complex. This will condition him to believe later, when is arrested for stealing a car, that society is against him and he is being persecuted.

5. Pick up everything he leaves laying around. Do everything for him so that he will be experienced in throwing all responsibility on others.

6. Let him read any printed matter he can get his hands on. Be careful that the silverware and drinking glasses are sterilized, but let his mind feast on garbage.

7. Quarrel frequently in the presence of your children. In this way they won't be so shocked when the home is broken up later.

8. Give a child all the spending money he wants. Never let him earn his own.

9. Satisfy his every craving for food, drink and comfort. See that every sensual desire is gratified.

10. Take his part against neighbors, teachers and policmen. They are all prejudiced against your child.

11. When he gets in real trouble, apologize for yourself by saying, "I never could do anything with him"

12. Prepare for a life of grief. You will be likely to have it.

From a Houston, Texas Newspaper

1

SELF-ESTEEM AND WHY IS IT SO IMPORTANT?

Self-Esteem is an inside job

Self-esteem is the integrated sum of self-confidence and self-respect. It's the conviction that you are competent to cope with life's challenges and worthy of happiness.
Nathaniel Branden

Self-esteem is the ability to feel good about yourself all the time no matter what, and the willingness for others to do the same. Self-esteem is the ability to allow others to experience themselves in your presence rather than impressing them with your presence. Self-esteem is pleasuring yourself and enjoying life in all that you do.
Patricia Dunrovy

Healthy self-esteem is not narcissistic, self-indulgent or arrogant. Healthy self-esteem means to appreciate the value of yourself as a unique human being with your own special talents and abilities
Reni Witt

Self-esteem is the reputation you have with yourself.
William Appleton

Self-esteem is the "price tag" we give ourselves. It is our perception of our worth. It is an overall judgment of ourselves. Self-esteem is self-regard.

Healthy self-esteem is an unconditional acceptance of you.

People with high self-esteem consider themselves worthy and view themselves as equal to others. They:

- do not pretend to be perfect

- recognize their limitations

- expect to grow and improve

- feel confident without being overbearing

- are not devastated by criticism

And, they are:

- not overly defensive when questioned

- mostly happy with themselves as they are

- not easily defeated by setbacks and obstacles able to accept and learn from their own mistakes

- unlikely to feel a need to put others down

- open and assertive in communicating their needs

- self-reliant and resourceful without refusing help from others

- not overly worried about failing or looking foolish

- not harshly or destructively critical of themselves

- able to laugh at themselves

Having a healthy self-esteem does not mean you have a "me first" attitude. People with an unhealthy self-esteem pretend they are more important than they are. People with a healthy self-esteem have no need to put themselves above others. They are happy with who they are and help others to feel the same.

I would like to dispel the myth that a person who is conceited has high self-esteem. This is not true. Conceit is but a whitewash to cover up low self-esteem. When you have high self-esteem, you don't waste time and energy impressing others because you already know you have value.

According to Denis Waitley, "*The Winning Generation*", "Being selfish, conceited and feeling superior to others has nothing to do with self-esteem. Individuals who act stuck-up and super cool most often have low self-esteem. Because they are insecure on the inside, they often show-off or sound off in their appearance and actions in order to attract attention and popularity. They are desperate for acceptance and have to make a loud or negative statement to try to feel important. Inside, they are crying out, 'Look at me. Please notice me!' On the other hand, some of us put ourselves down and talk negatively about ourselves thinking that others will like us more if we raise them up by tearing ourselves down. True self-esteem is a deep-down, inside-the-skin feeling of your own worth. Self-esteem is not based on looks, athletic or academic ability, or being the hit of the party. If you have self-esteem, you have no need to make comparisons, act important, put others down or put yourself down."

According to many specialists on self–esteem there are some key ingredients children and adults need to possess to have healthy self-esteem.

KEY INGREDIENTS OF SELF-ESTEEM

1. A Sense of Physical and Emotional Safety: This means that you are not fearful of being harmed, hurt or put down. You feel safe in your school, home, and neighborhood. You know what is expected and are able to trust and depend on individuals and situations.

2. A Sense of Identity: You develop an accurate and realistic self-description. You know your strengths and weaknesses.

3. A Sense of Belonging: You feel accepted, approved, appreciated and respected by others. You feel valued by important people in your life.

4. A Sense of Competence: You feel capable of achieving what is important to you. When you feel sure of yourself

3

and your abilities, you feel in charge of your life. You're aware of your strengths and, in areas where you are less capable, you lead with your strengths.

5. A Sense of Purpose: You have mission in life. You set and achieve realistic goals that are important to you. You are self-motivated and have a clear direction.

What is the Difference Between Self-esteem And Self-image?

We have thousands of images of ourselves. You have an image of how you are as a cook, how you are as a golfer, how you are as a mother, as a father; a driver, a listener, a writer, a parent and a teacher — many different images.

> PEOPLE WITH HEALTHY SELF-ESTEEM HAVE A REALISTIC AWARENESS OF THEMSELVES AND OF THEIR ABILITIES

Your self-esteem is an average of all of those images. If you have many poor images of yourself, you will have overall low self-esteem. It's similar to a report card where you get individual grades for each subject, which then get totaled into an average.

REPORT CARD

MOTHER   B
GOLFER   F
ATHLETE B
COOK   D
TEACHER A

For example, you may have great confidence in yourself as a writer but feel incompetent as a speaker. So, when you are put in a situation where you have to speak, you may feel threatened and insecure. This doesn't mean you have low self-esteem; it just means in this one area you feel less confident. However if you are in a speaking situation all day, everyday, and feel insecure, never confident, it affects your self-esteem. Compare this to children who are in school seven hours a day, five days a week, and are always experiencing failure. They will begin to believe they are failures.

Why is Healthy/High Self-esteem so Important

Your child's judgment of himself influences:

- the kinds of friends he chooses or attracts
- how he gets along with others
- the kind of person he marries
- how productive he will be
- his ability to cope with ups and downs in life
- his ability to persist in spite of obstacles
- his creativity, integrity, and stability
- whether he will be a leader or a follower

It affects:

- Attitude
- Enthusiasm
- Health
- Courage
- Moods
- Patience
- Schoolwork
- Physical appearance
- Energy
- Initiative

A person's feeling of self-worth forms the core of his personality and determines how he will make use of his aptitudes and abilities.

Why is it so important to like and accept yourself? It is important because it affects everything a parent or a child does. Every decision made is based on one's self-esteem. Every interaction with somebody is based on self-esteem. Will you go into the staff lounge to eat lunch when you don't know anyone? Will you stand up for yourself when put down? Comments people make to you are interpreted according to your self-esteem.

Suppose I came up to you and said, "That is an interesting necklace you are wearing." What would your first thought be? Would it be "Why did she pick the word 'interesting'? Does that mean she doesn't like it? Does she think it's ugly? Oh no, now everyone will look at it and think I wear ugly jewelry!" or would it be "Yes, it is very interesting and unique. I do have good taste in jewelry. I am so glad you pointed it out in front of everyone because now when people come up to see it I can teach people how to better accessorize with jewelry." ☺ See the difference?

Did you know that 37% of American adults suffer from poor self-esteem? That's one out of every three people. Think about that. If you are sitting between two people, one of the three of you is suffering from poor self-esteem. In kindergarten, 80% of the kids have high self-esteem. Not bad. By the time they get to fifth grade only 20% have high self-esteem. When they get to high school, only 5% have high self-esteem. By the time they reach adulthood, forget it, there is no hope! Actually, I lied, there is plenty of hope. The great thing about self-esteem is that it doesn't matter whether you are 7, 17, or 77; if you don't like yourself, it is never too late to change. If you are not happy with yourself you can change! It takes work, it takes time but YOU CAN DO IT. I was about 25 when I started to really make progress in building my confidence. And there is no stopping me now! ☺

How is Self-esteem Formed?

The foundations of self-esteem are laid early in life when infants develop attachments with the adults who are responsible for them. Children come to feel loved and accepted from being loved and accepted by people they look up to. As young children learn to trust their parents to satisfy their basic needs, they gradually feel wanted, valued, and loved.

The first five years of our lives are the most critical years in the development of your self-esteem. Children, like sponges, have a tremendous capacity to absorb unlimited amounts of information that come in through the form of a parent's body language, tone of voice, hugs, and labels. By age five, children have collected enough information about themselves to form an overall estimation of their worth. During their early years, young children's self-esteem is based largely on their perceptions of how the important adults in their lives judge them.

Dorothy Briggs, author of *Your Child's Self-Esteem*, says that in the past, people would build houses from whatever materials were available to them. If mud was in abundance, they would build their homes from mud. If straw or brick were available, they would use that. Children build their self-esteem from whatever is available to them in their environment. If they hear nothing but negative comments and have negative experiences in their environment, that is what they build their self-esteem with. If they are surrounded by lots of encouragement, are nourished when family members show they love and value one another, when they hear positive comments and have positive experiences, then that is what they are going to build their self-esteem with.

So ask yourself:

What happens in your home environment?

What are your children using to form their self-esteem?

Are we as parents:

- Allowing for differences
- Trusting

- Communicating openly

- Listening

- Showing respect and understanding

- Spending time with each other

- Looking for opportunities to be encouraging

- Having a sense of humor

- Recognizing that it is acceptable to make mistakes

- Finding ways to support each other

- Sharing responsibilities

Children value themselves only to the extent that they feel valued by the important people in their lives. In families where these things happen, children feel good about themselves. They feel valuable and competent. They feel like they belong.

Every remark positive or negative accumulates and forms a mirror. We hold this

SELF-ESTEEM COMES FROM THE QUALITY OF RELATIONSHIPS THAT EXIST BETWEEN THE CHILD AND THOSE WHO PLAY A SIGNIFICANT ROLE IN HIS LIFE.

mirror up to our child and say, "Here is how I see you." A child uses this mirror to get an image of himself and tends to believe these reflections. If everything they hear is negative, they will see a very distorted image of themselves. It is as if each negative remark puts a crack in the mirror. Adults are the 'psychological mirror' a child uses to build his identity. As infants, they gather thousands of impressions about themselves through adults' body language, actions, attitudes and words. Like a mirror, adults can reflect beauty and uniqueness or flaws and shortcomings and these reflections have a powerful impact on a child's sense of self. What are you reflecting?

Concrete Ways to Explain Self-esteem

Self-esteem is a very abstract concept so it is hard to go up to a child and say, "How is your self-esteem today?" A child has no idea what you're talking about. Let's look at two concrete ways to explain and understand self-esteem.

The Computer

One way to describe self-esteem is to think of it as a computer. Your self-esteem is housed in your brain. Your brain is like a computer. Whatever goes into the computer comes out on the screen. If you have a disc containing math and you put that into the computer, math comes out onto the screen, not reading or spelling. In the same way, whatever goes into your child's mind comes out in his behavior/actions. Every time your child hears things like:

"You are so stupid."

"Oh, you're so lazy. Can't you do anything right?"

"You know, you're as bad as your father."

"What? Did you forget your brain today?"

"You never get anything done on time."

"Why can't you be more like your sister?"

"You just don't think."

"Can't you get anything through your thick head?"

"You'll be the death of me yet!"

"I don't know why I put up with you?"

his computer is programmed. When they do a task, they automatically check with their subconscious /self-esteem and their brain spits out what has been programmed. For example, "Oh, no. I can't do that. Remember...I'm lazy." "Oh, no. I'm not going to be able to do that because I'm not as good as my sister."

When you put garbage in, garbage comes back out. People often say, "Oh, that is so over-simplified. It can't be that simple." Here is a perfect example. A mother and son were in a bakery. The little boy wanted to carry the cake that his mother had just bought. He cried "Oh, Mommy! Mommy! Mommy! Please can I carry the cake? Please!" His mother responded, "No. The last time I let you carry it you dropped it. You're not going to carry that cake." "Oh, Mommy! Please! Please! Please!" Sometimes, if a child begs long enough the parent will give in. In this case the mother did. She said, "All right! Here! Fine! Carry the cake! Promise me you won't drop it. Don't you dare drop that cake! You'd better not drop that cake!" Can you guess what the little boy did? Right! He dropped the cake. Whose fault do you think that was? In this instance it was the mother's fault. Now, let's not judge this mother. She is not a bad mother who woke up in the morning wondering how she could sabotage her child. She simply did what many people do. She emphasized the behavior she didn't want rather than emphasize the behavior she did want. The mom got back exactly what she programmed in. She didn't say, "Use two hands. Be careful. I know you can do it", so all the child was thinking about was the negative.

If someone said to you right now, "Whatever you do, don't think about your left foot, don't think about it!" What do you think the first thing that you are going to think about will be? Very often, we program the negatives in without realizing it. This cartoon illustrates how innocently we program children.

Notice in this illustration that there is a little boy carrying his plate level until his mother says, "Don't tilt the plate." The brain thinks in pictures or images, not words. Can you picture "DON'T?" Think of a parent who has a challenge with the child who wets the bed. After tucking him in, the parent says, "Don't wet your bed tonight." What will the child visualize? A much more effective statement would be "Let's see if you can keep your bed dry tonight." This statement conjures up the image the parent wants and the child is left with a positive image rather than a negative one. You cannot teach a child to "NOT". Not to run, not to speak, not to ride a bike. They already know how to do these things. You have to teach them what you want them to do, not what you want them to stop. We need to stop programming them with negative images and labels.

Negative Labeling

Negative Labeling is when we attach an adjective to a child that in the adult's perception matches the child's behavior or actions. Example: brat, slob, lazy, selfish, rude and stupid. How often are we programming in the negative, "You'll fall." "You'll slip!" "You're going to make a mess." "You're hopeless!" "You're as bad as your uncle." We don't realize how often we label. Take a moment to think about it. When you introduce your children to someone, have you said, "Let me introduce you to my oldest one, or, this is the baby of the family...and she is going to drive me to the grave." ☺ We introduce them with labels. We may say something like, "This is my shy one" and wonder why they run and hide behind our legs. We've given them a label. When you go into a restaurant, what do you say to your children before you go in? "Whatever you do don't act like wild animals!" instead of saying something like "We are

> CHILDREN WILL TAILOR THEIR ACTIONS TO FIT THE ROLE ASSIGNED THEM – POSITIVE OR NEGATIVE

going into the restaurant and you need to use your indoor voice, let me hear your indoor voice". Or, "Your friends are coming over, don't act like your greedy little self again."

Instead, "Your friends are coming over, what toys are you willing to share while they are here?" Or maybe, "I'd better not get a bad report from the babysitter when I get home." Instead you could say, "I am looking forward to hearing from the sitter about how well you listened, did your homework and went to bed on time."

When we put negative thoughts into a child's mind, they become integrated in his behavior. So be specific about the behavior that you want from a child. If you're specific about positive behavior, you will get positive behavior. Children tailor their actions to fit the role adults assign to them. It is done in schools, in corporations and in our homes. Our own parents did it to us. We are given a role, and we lived up to that role. A clear example of this happened one year when I was teaching six severely and emotionally handicapped boys. I had taken over teaching them in September after they had been through three teachers during a six-week summer school program. The boys had even broken the arm of their last teacher. They were obviously a challenging group. My colleagues would approach me and say, "Oh my gosh, you got that class? You've got the worst class in the whole school! Did you wear your combat gear? You're never going to be able to handle these kids." They made these comments in earshot of my students.

On my first day my introduction to the class was, *"This is going to be a great year and, we're going to be successful; it doesn't matter what happened last year. We are going to start off fresh and with a clean slate."* One of my students, Bobby, raised his hand and said, "Didn't you hear about us? We are the meanest, baddest class in the whole school. Did you hear what we did to the last teacher? Wait until you see what we are going to do to you." My first inner thought was, "Oh No, perhaps it is time for a career change!" What was so sad and amazing to me was that he said it with so much pride! That was the image he was given and he was going to live up to it! My first challenge was to change that image by changing the information that was stored in the class's "computer". Any time someone came into my room, like the principal, the nurse, or another teacher, I would say, "Come on in! Let me introduce you to one of the best-behaved classes in the whole school!" I introduced each one of the students. After a couple of times of hearing this, Bobby approached me and said, "Mrs. Brittingham, why are you lying to those people"? My comments didn't match Bobby's image, which is when I realized that saying positive comments to someone with low self-esteem is not enough to change them. It is important to back these comments with proof. Such proof would be pointing out successful experiences or behaviors that are happening on a daily basis. From then on, I made it a point to recognize Bobby's small successes. I began to continually point out that he was using words to get his needs met rather than throwing punches, and that demonstrated good self-control. That is the way a student behaves in the best-behaved class. Sometimes I would have to look for the smallest improvements such as: "You have your name on the paper, that's a start"

After just two weeks of introducing my class in this manner and backing it up with proof, my principal walked in the door. As I was walking over to do my positive introduction of the class once again, Bobby cut in front of me and said to the principal, "I want to introduce you to the best-behaved class in the whole school and I'm one of the kids in it!" What I started to successfully do was to change what was in Bobby's computer. It would be nice to think that from that point on Bobby was a perfect child but that would be lying to you. It was only the beginning. It took one and one half years to get Bobby mainstreamed into a regular class. Changing what was inside was just the beginning. I had to give them experiences to back up what I said to get them to believe it—ultimately changing their behavior.

Be aware of the messages you are sending by giving a child negative labels. Remember, "Negative labeling is disabling."

Give your child positive labels to live up to. For example, "I saw you share your candy with your sister, how generous!" "I noticed you helped your mother with dinner without her asking; how thoughtful that was!" "You called when you knew you would be late; that was very responsible." A child will strive to keep the positive label and *in order for that to happen they first have to know the specific behavior you are looking for that gives them the positive label.*

IALAC sign

A more effective way to explain self-esteem to children and adults is to use the IALAC demonstration.

IALAC stands for "I am lovable and capable". We all need to feel loved. We need to know that somebody cares about us and loves us unconditionally. We need to feel capable of reaching the goals that we set for ourselves, of making decisions for ourselves, of learning the multiplication tables, or graduating from high school.

IALAC is a visual example that helps make self-esteem more concrete rather than abstract, making it easier to understand. This is how the IALAC sign works. Wear a sign, an 8 1/2"x11" piece of paper around your neck that has written on it, "I am lovable and capable."

Tell your child, "This sign represents how you feel about yourself. It gets bigger and bigger when people show they love and care about you, when people listen to you, when your opinions matter, or when they play with you and spend time with you. But when things don't go so well, when no one has time for you, when people make fun of you, when no one seems to play with you or care about you, then your sign gets smaller and smaller. Each time a negative incident occurs it rips away a piece of your sign."

14

Then as you tell your child the story about Michelle, demonstrate what happens to her sign. ***Riiiiip! Rip! Rip!***

Michelle is in the third grade. She woke up one morning and her mother said, "Michelle! Michelle! Get out of bed you lazy head." **Rip!**

"How many times do I have to wake you up?" Michelle quickly got up, jumped out of bed and ran to the bathroom to get dressed. She banged on the door and her sister said "Oh, drop dead. Nothing in here is going to make you look any better." **Rip!**

Michelle went downstairs and her mother said, "You're going to school looking like that? Oh! I'd be so embarrassed. **Rip!**

"Go upstairs and change those clothes." **Rip!**

She ran upstairs and changed her clothes, went back downstairs and her mother said, "No time for breakfast. You're late and it is your own fault." **Rip!**

She rushed out to catch the bus. Her mother yelled, "Michelle! Get back here! You forgot your lunch. You'd forget your head if it wasn't attached." **Rip!**

Michelle went to get her lunch then ran to the bus. When she got there, all of the kids started making fun of her, "Oh! Here she is, the four-eyed geek." **Rip!**

She got on the bus and all of the kids put their feet up on the seat so that she couldn't sit with them. **Rip!**

The driver said, "You put your feet down and let her sit there." Then another kid said "Ewe. I hope I don't catch any diseases from her." **Rip!**

She arrived in the classroom. Since all of the buses hadn't arrived yet, the teacher let the children play for a while.

Michelle and Suzy started building with Legos and

*then Betty came over and said, "Ewe, you play with Michelle; she wears those cheap smelly clothes." **Rip!***

*They both just left and Michelle was left to play by herself. **Rip!***

*She heard one of the teachers talking to another teacher. The teacher said, "Well, you know that Michelle? She just isn't as quick as the other kids. She certainly is not as smart as her sister." **Rip!***

*In reading class, Michelle was asked to read out loud. She made a mistake and all the kids in the class laughed. One kid said, "Oh, the retard is reading again." **Rip!***

*At lunch everyone was having spaghetti and Michelle was excited because spaghetti is one of her favorite things so she went to get her spaghetti tray. One of the kids stuck out his foot and tripped her. Everyone in the cafeteria laughed. **Rip!***

*Then Michelle went to sit down and everyone moved toward the end of the table because they didn't want to sit next to her. **Rip!***

*FINALLY, at the end of the day Michelle was excited because she played soccer and had a game that day. She was a really good soccer player. Her dad said that he would try to be there to see her play. She was excited because her dad was always so busy at work that he had never gone to one of her games before. She couldn't wait for him to come. He never showed. **Rip!***

*And it didn't matter. It was just a stupid soccer game. She thought to herself, "I'm not that good anyhow." **Rip!***

*She couldn't wait to get home and tell her mom all about her day and everything that happened. She went in the house and started talking to her mom who said, "Michelle, can't you see I'm busy right now?" **Rip!***

*She was always too busy for Michelle but never too busy to talk on that stupid phone. **Rip!***

*Her mother told her that grandma was coming over. She was so excited! She loved her grandmother because her grandmother really loved her. She really listened to her. She paid lots of attention to her. She gave her lots of hugs and kisses. Michelle decided that she would help her mother set the table. While setting the table Michelle accidently dropped one of the glasses and broke it. Her mother said, "Oh, Michelle...get out of here. You're so clumsy." **Rip!** "I'd rather do it myself." **Rip!***

*She was excited when her grandmother arrived. They sat on the couch and talked about Michelle's day and about her soccer game, then all of a sudden, Michelle's mother brought the baby in the room and everyone started looking at the baby saying, "Oh, the baby is so cute. Oh I want to hold the baby!" Michelle thought, "That stupid baby. They forget about me whenever that baby is around." **Rip!***

*They went in and started eating dinner. Michelle's mother made mashed potatoes. Mashed potatoes were her most favorite food in the whole world. She went to take a second helping and her father said, "Boy, Michelle, if you keep taking second helpings like that, pretty soon you're going to be as big as your mother." **Rip!.***

Can you imagine how Michelle felt about herself then? Did you ever stop to think of how all these seemingly unimportant comments shatter a child's self-esteem? And yet, the adults who make these comments usually do not think twice about them. But the child who hears them never forgets.

Paul's Story

When Paul was younger he was very tall for his age.

He was nearly 5'2" when he was in 3rd and 4th grade. He hated the fact that he was tall when he was younger. Now that Paul is older and he is more comfortable with his height, he is often asked, why he hated being tall when he was younger. His response is, "Because I remember when the coach would line us up for team practice, he would say, "Hey you! The tall goon. You follow up the back." And everybody on the team laughed. Even I laughed but then I went home and cried because I wondered how many people thought I looked like a tall goon." Paul tried to hide the fact that he was tall by slouching and he had poor posture. It took eight years of positive comments and positive experiences to counteract that one negative statement, a statement the adult didn't think twice about. But Paul never forgot.

How often do we make careless comments, not realizing the lasting effect they will have on a child or adult? It is similar to a piece of crystal. We may carelessly or accidentally knock the crystal off the shelf and it will break into several pieces. It takes a lot of time, and patience to put the crystal back together; even then it will still be fragile. Adults often make comments accidentally that shatter a child's self-esteem. It takes a lot of positive comments and positive experiences to counteract one negative comment. It would be easier if we would be more careful with the words we say to begin with.

Although children appear to bounce back after you rip their IALAC sign to shreds, and they come back with another sign, the new sign is significantly smaller. When their sign becomes very small, they fear taking risks. Inwardly they think, "You want me to go and make friends with the kids down the street? What, are you kidding me? What if I get rejected? I can't afford to have another piece ripped out of my sign". "You want me to try out for the soccer team? Are you kidding me? What if I don't make it? It's going to rip the last shred of self-esteem that I have." "You want me to try harder and study for a test and act like I care? I can't afford to."

We are going to explore how adults rip a child's sign and what adults can do to add pieces back on. However, keep in mind children need to take control over their own sign not permitting others to rip it. How to achieve this will be discussed in chapter seven.

Jokes and Ripping

We live in a society where nearly every night we watch television sitcoms. Actors get laughs by putting somebody else down or teasing them about one of their flaws or mistakes. A lot of friendly relationships (especially between males) are based on banter, which may be fine if the person is not feeling sensitive that day. People often ask, "Can we ever just joke around or tease our children, after all, sometimes we are just joking? My reply: "Does the person on the receiving end know for sure it is a joke with no hidden meaning? Are you sure that person won't be hurt by your words?"

Let's pretend you have beautiful naturally brown hair and you are at a party with your spouse and friends. If someone approached you and said, "You have the ugliest green hair I've ever seen." You know your hair is not green so is that going to affect your self-esteem? Is it going to rip pieces out of your IALAC sign? Probably not, since your hair is obviously not green. They could joke all night about your hair and it is not going to bother you because you know it is not true. On the other hand, what if someone said, "Hey, I see you are finally reading that parenting book. You sure could use it." Is this joking comment going to affect your self-esteem? Most likely it will. This is not because what was said was true, but because there is not one parent that at some point didn't question whether or not they were a good parent. Could they do a better job? Should they do this differently or that differently? With that comment/joke a piece of your IALAC sign was just ripped even though the person said they were only joking.

Now imagine on your way home your spouse said, "Honey, wasn't that funny that she picked you out of all those people. How did she know you are a bad parent and need this book?" Now, he was just joking but do you know what? That "joke" just ripped a little piece out of your sign as a parent. What happens next? The next day when you bring your child into school, everyone is standing around in a circle talking. When you approach, they stop talking. What is your first thought? "Oh, Oh, they're all talking about what Joann said last night. They think I'm a poor parent." There goes a piece of your sign. Three pieces have been carelessly torn off because of one "joke". We have no way of knowing how sensitive someone is on any given day, and they are not likely to come up to you and say, "Please don't tease me today, I am feeling sensitive."

When I was growing up, I always believed that I had a very big nose. My brothers would joke around about it but I would just tease them back about one of their many flaws. One day somebody approached me and said, "Oh, MaryAnn! You are a spitting image of your grandmother. You look just like her." I'm sure they meant that as a compliment but although my grandmother was a wonderful woman, she had a nose like you wouldn't believe! The next day when my brothers teased me, instead of laughing and teasing them back, I went into my room and cried my eyes out. I wrote a list of 100 ways I was going make enough money to get a nose job. I'm still saving up. That is really why I am writing this book!!! ☺

Here are some examples of what can be done at home or at school:

1: Do the IALAC demonstration.

2. Select a signal word (or secret code word)such as "**Rip**".

3. Use a "secret code word" to signal to others that what they are saying is not funny—but hurts.

4. When someone says something that may be funny at first but then keeps it up and it starts to bother you, you simply say, "**Rip**" and all teasing and joking must stop. This means child-to-child and adult-to-child and adult-to-adult. It is a quick, easy way to let others know to stop. It is more effective than going into a long lecture with your children; instead you can say, "You just ripped a piece of her sign. We don't rip pieces in this house. We add pieces on."

Just a warning though; when you first do this with your kids they will say, "**Rip**" to everything you say. Clean your room, "**Rip**", do your homework, "**Rip**." In fact, even when this is done for adults at the work place, they often start initially using it as a joke.

SELECT AND USE A CODE WORD TO PREVENT HURTFUL JOKING

One father had set the "Rip" idea up with his family. Later that week he was attending his 14-year-old son's basketball game. He was in the bleachers yelling, "Get your hands up, run faster, get those hands up!" The son turned to him gestured as if he was ripping a piece of paper and mouthed, "Riiiiipppp!" At first the father was puzzled. He thought that he was only reminding him or encouraging him. But to the child he was saying "You're not doing it right." When we keep reminding or nagging others what we are really saying is, "I don't trust that you will remember on your own. I don't have faith in you to do it."

Pose this question to yourself: Do you think that the 14-year-old boy would have said to his dad on the way home in the car, "Dad, I need to talk with you? Something is bothering me. It hurts my feelings and insults me when you scream reminders to me during the game." That's very doubtful. However, with the "rip" signal, the son had a quick easy way to let the father know what he was feeling.

Take Control of the Inner Computer

The first thing we need to teach children to do is take

control of their inner computer. Everything somebody says does not have to get stored in their computer as fact, as truth. Children think everything an adult says is true. Why? Think of a two-year old. They think of adults as powerful "Gods" that treat them as they deserve to be treated. Here is their logic: What they say about me is what I am. They know when to feed me, they know what I should eat, they know how to make a cut feel better, and they know what to do when I am sick. They know everything, so when they say "what a stupid idea", "you're a loser, you'll never amount to anything", they must be right because they are right about everything else.

Your children have a choice, just as you have a choice not to store all information in your computer. When somebody says something to you, you decide whether or not you want that information stored as fact. Pretend I went up to a woman named Michelle and said, "You know, Michelle, you're one very stupid woman." What can Michelle do about a comment like this? She has a choice. She can say, "How did she figure that out so fast? It takes most people ten minutes!" Or, Michelle can say, "This lady doesn't know me. She doesn't know what a dedicated parent I am, what a caring person I am, so what she is saying is not true. I'm not going to store it in my computer as fact". Just as Michelle has a choice, we all have a choice. Your children have a choice, only they haven't been taught that yet. When you get angry, – and we all get angry and lose our temper and say things that we regret – children take that and store it as fact. "See. I am stupid. Even mom and dad say I am." We have to teach them that adults are human—we have bad days and sometimes say negative things. That doesn't mean it is true and should be stored in our computer.

A good way to make this idea concrete for kids is to cook spaghetti with them. Explain to them that you put the spaghetti in the water. You need the water to cook the spaghetti but when it's cooked you let the water drain out because the only part that nourishes us is the spaghetti. The only part that helps you grow is that spaghetti. If you leave the water in the pot, it will make the spaghetti soggy and it will be no good. So you let the water drain out.

The water is your criticism or negative labels. I'll listen to your criticism but if it doesn't help me grow, if it doesn't make me a better person, I'm going to let it drain out. Calling me stupid doesn't teach me how to improve; it just gives me an unhelpful negative label. I'm going to let that drain out, keeping it in my mind will only make me feel worse. If you tell me specifically, what I need to do to improve, I might keep that in mind and work on it because that may help me grow to be a better person. We need to let kids know that they have a choice and we, as adults, have a choice. We don't have to store and believe everything our parents, boss, or spouse says.

Apologize

Remember we all make mistakes, but kids are forgiving. Let them know you made a mistake and apologize. Say the words "I'm sorry." Let your child know you are working to change that behavior. This helps them to realize:

1. They are not a bad person

2. They are still loved and worthwhile.

3. It is OK to make mistakes (even mommy and daddy make mistakes)

Apologizing also models for your children what they should do when they make a mistake. It teaches them to take responsibility for their behavior.

"We make butterflies by feeding caterpillars, not by trying to paste wings on them"

Foster Cline

Parents are not totally responsible
for a child's degree of self-esteem,
but they play a major role in his
initial view of himself and are
significant in his life
for many years.

The trait you least like in your child
is often the same trait in yourself
that you reject.

Dorothy Briggs

2

☺ ☺ ☺

BEHAVIORS AND THEIR IMPACT
ON CHILDREN

Getting rid of bad habits is like peeling an onion;
it must be done one layer at a time.

We are going to go through a list of things that happen at home that affect a child's self-esteem in a negative way.

As we go through this list you may be tempted to throw this book across the room and say, "My God! It's too late. I've destroyed my child!" Don't worry; it is never too late to change. However, if you don't do any of the things indicated, wonderful! Give yourself a pat on the back! If you do all of them, don't beat yourself up; pick one thing that you want to work on to change. Only do one thing at a time, otherwise you will get overwhelmed and give up. (Then you won't recommend my book, I won't make any money, my self-esteem will crumble and I'll never get my nose job!!! ☺)

This list is important to go through because you cannot solve or stop a problem unless you're aware of it first. Awareness is the first step to change. Go though the list and select which behavior is most important to you to change. You may want to start with an easy one first so you can experience success. You will spend the first week just catching yourself after the fact. Then you will move to stopping yourself midstream and finally to one day deleting the behavior before it happens.

1. Telling a child to shut up:

- Shut up! I can't think when you are babbling on and on.

- Shut your mouth this minute or I'll close it for you!

- Shut up and go to bed.

- Just shut up and get out of here.

- Oh shut up, you don't know what you are talking about.

- Shut up and get out of my face.

- Can't you see I'm busy right now? Shut up!

Telling a child to shut up is one of the things we don't realize we do. How would you respond if your child told you to shut up? (They may be modeling your behavior.)"Shut up" is terribly harsh and hurtful. Saying, "be quiet," means the same thing and it is not as harsh. Alternatives to shut up are:" Please be quiet!" "Please stop talking, I need to think" "I am very annoyed right now; you need to be silent" "It is time to be silent and go to sleep."

How many of us would say shut up to our friends? How many of us would have friends left if we treated them like we treat our children? Isn't it funny that we often treat outsiders better than our own family members? Think back to when you were younger and your mother was screaming like a banshee at you for something you had done. Suddenly the phone rings, your mom picks it up and in a calm sweet voice says "Hello". Now doesn't that send a message that says outsiders are worthy of your kindness and respect but your children are not?

2. Talking negatively about kids in front of them:

The funny thing about children is that when you talk to

them they don't hear you. But when you mention their name to someone else and they are in another room, they hear every word you say.

Think of all the things that are said about children when they are supposedly not listening. Then remember their acute listening powers, – like hearing a candy bar getting unwrapped from 50 yards away! Parents forget with toddlers that although they haven't started to say many words, they understand enormous amounts of what is being said.

©Lynn Johnson Productions, Inc./Distributed by United Feature Syndicate, Inc.

Dr. Wayne Dyer, author of *The Sky's The Limit*, tells the story about when he was in grade school. His teacher stood by the door talking to the principal. He heard the teacher say, "Wayne is a scurby elephant." He was very upset. He went home told his mother and she was outraged. She called the principal and said, "How dare you call my son a scurby elephant!" The principal had no idea what she was talking about and went on to explain that she and the teacher were having a private conversation and the teacher said, "Wayne was a disturbing element in the classroom." But Wayne heard, "scurby elephant".

There is a story about a father who took his son for some testing because the school had requested it. When the testing was done the father and psychologist were discussing the results while the son played in the back of the room. The psychologist said, "Your son is brain damaged. He won't be able to read, write, or be a productive member of society so you might as well just institutionalize him." The doctor figured the boy could not understand this so it didn't matter if he was within earshot or not. Later that night when the father was tucking his son in, the boy asked, "Dad, would I be better off dead?"

On the other hand, if you speak positively about your children in front of other people it would have a very powerful and positive impact on their self-esteem. Just think about how your child would feel when you tell dad, on his arrival home, how helpful the child was to a neighbor by taking her groceries in without even being asked.

3. Using Negative nicknames:

Having names like "Fat Albert", "Bozo", "Stretch", "Lard boy", "Shorty" and so on, isn't helpful because they give a negative nickname for a child to live up to. When I was growing up I went through a very clumsy stage, breaking everything in sight and hurting myself. As a result my name at home became "Calamity Jane." That was my nickname. So, when I walked into the room everyone would say, "Hold your glasses. Here comes Calamity Jane. You don't know what she'll break." The more they said things like that, the longer I stayed in that clumsy stage. Give your children positive names to live up to like: "Sunshine", "Smiles", and "Cuddles".

4. Comparing siblings:

If you have more than one child you will most likely identify with this. Say your first child was a "model child", and you did everything right. You thought parenting was going to be so easy. Along comes the second child. SURPRISE! You swear there was a mix up at the hospital because this child couldn't possibly be from the same parents. The two children are so different you start to compare:

"How come this one gives me so much trouble?"

"How come he is always having temper tantrums?"

"How come she doesn't get good grades like her brother?"

"How come he is so shy and afraid of anything new, yet

his sister is so outgoing?"

Parents often ask, "How can two children with the same parents be so different." The answer to this is that no two children ever have the same parents or same family. The first child has a much different family from the second child. The first child did not have to share your attention with anyone. Even if you are doing your best to give all of the children equal attention, they are still competing and comparing themselves to their siblings. They are searching to find their place in the family.

Also what you learned in parenting the first child makes you different parents with the second or third child, not to mention that children come into the world with their own unique temperament, personality, moods, interest and talents. Just because one child needs more attention than the other doesn't make them bad. Just because one child is less active than the other doesn't make them lazy. If one child uses their musical talent and the other doesn't, this does not make them wrong. Comparing one child to another is simply not fair. They're just different and they have different ways of getting their needs met. It is important to realize this; otherwise, you may easily become frustrated with them.

Many of you know enough not to say to your child, "Why couldn't you be more like your brother? He is so motivated and smart; he doesn't give me any trouble." Yet even while you may never say these words, it comes across in your tone of voice, the amount of patience you have with one child versus the other, the amount of time you want to spend with one child, and the amount of affection and praise you give. In other words, it comes across in actions as well as words.

A friend of mine has three children. Her youngest one is a handful to say the least. She will frequently go on about how Sarah is not like the first two. "They grew up without any problems. You didn't even know they were around. But not Sarah, everyday she is in a crisis. I love her just the same, but boy she can drive me crazy!" Now there is no doubt the mom loves her daughter. However, by consistently comparing Sarah to the older two, mom gets frustrated. Sarah never measures up and is made to be the "bad child". While the mom says she loves Sarah, her body language, tone of voice, amount of patience, and free time spent with Sarah is undoubtedly different from what the older two get.

Remind yourself. It's OK that children are different; different is not bad. It is what makes each of us unique

5. Interrupting:

How would you feel if you were talking at a party and your spouse came up, grabbed you by the arm, and said "Come on. We've got to go!" and pulled you right away from your conversation? What would you do? Divorce him or her? Chances are you would get very annoyed and possibly angry. Yet we think nothing of cutting our children short when they are telling us a story or talking. When they are busy talking to somebody we just interrupt. "OK, enough! Go to bed." or, "Did you clean your room?" When children talk to us, you know it takes them three thousand words or more to say what could be said in one hundred words or less, thus it takes them twenty-five minutes to say what could be said in five.

So, you pretend you're listening "Oh, really. Uh-huh. Uh-huh" but your distraction or disinterest shows and gives your child the impression that you really don't care about what they are saying.

Some alternatives

- "I'd like to hear what you have to say; however, I don't have time and can't give you my full attention right now. Can you tell me during dinner?

- "I'd like to hear more about that. Can you tell me

before you go to bed?" Be sure you go back and ask even if it's three hours later!

- "We are short on time and you sound excited to share this, could you tell me the abbreviated version for now?"

- Or you could say, "I would like to listen to your story while I fold these clothes. Is that OK with you?" However if they say no, be prepared to stop folding.

6. Giving orders:

Sometimes parents forget the words "please" and "thank you". Remember, you are always role models. Monkey see, monkey do. If your child doesn't hear you saying "Please clean up your room," or, "Thank you for taking out the garbage," they will not say please and thank you.

7. Breaking promises:

This is a tough one because we don't realize how often we break promises to children. We might not actually say the words "I promise," but if a child approaches you and says, "Mom, after dinner can we go to the park?" and you say, "Maybe, I'll think about it," or "I'll see." What does that mean to a child?

- I have to play lawyer and convince her is it a good idea.

- Yes, we are going to the park after dinner.

- If I am good during dinner, will she will say "yes".

Then when you say "No", the child retaliates with, "That's not fair, I was good. You lied, you said we could go!" And a full-blown temper tantrum erupts. Instead of saying "later" or "I'll see", just say "You can ask me after dinner and I'll let you know." This statement helps reduce the child's misperceptions of "maybe".

Give the child a specific time or day to ask you. "Can

Tommy sleep over on Saturday?" "Ask me Friday night and I will give you my answer."

Sometimes we do promise. We may say, "Yes, this weekend I'll take you out to get that new pair of sneakers". Subsequently, the car breaks down or you run out of money and it prevents you from being able to take them. You then tell them, "I'm sorry. We'll go next weekend." This simply doesn't fly with your child because he already announced to all his friends that he was getting new sneakers this weekend. Now he fears all his friends will consider him a liar. What follows is, he pesters you all week about getting those rotten sneakers until you are ready to strangle him. Because of your frustration, you end up saying, "If you mention sneakers one more time, you'll never see them. Just forget the sneakers".

You sometimes need to get into your children's minds and think as they would think. "If mom or dad broke the first promise, they'll probably break the second unless I keep reminding them". Now this has nothing to do with reality (unless you break promises repeatedly). How do you counteract this? One way to let your child know you understand that he is afraid you will forget is to go with him to the calendar and mark the day you will take him. When and if he asks again, you can simply state that if he looks on the calendar he can see there are only X number of days until he gets his sneakers - and then hope like crazy that nothing happens to spoil your plans!

Circumstances beyond your control do happen. A good lesson for children to learn is that things don't always go as planned. Make sure you take the time to explain why Plan A didn't work and that it wasn't anyone's fault, and together make plan B. He will still be disappointed but will better understand why he can't get his sneakers this weekend.

If this happens once in a while, children understand but if it repeatedly happens, they will start to mistrust you.

8. Overprotection:

Parents love their children so much they want to protect them from every possible danger and heartache. However, overprotection can undermine a child's self respect. Constantly watching and warning your child about the dangers of the world or doing things for your child that they can do for themselves, sends the message that they are not competent.

NEVER DO FOR KIDS WHAT THEY CAN DO FOR THEMSELVES.

9. Comparing abilities:

We have a very competitive society. Everybody wants to be a winner. Nobody wants to be a loser. What we need to teach our children, as well as ourselves, is not to measure our weaknesses and strengths against other people but to look inside ourselves and see where our talents lie and how we can best use and improve them. Just because someone excels in one area does not mean they are better than another; they are just better in that one area.

Be the best you can be, not what someone else can be.

10. Allowing exclusion:

The scenario typically goes like this. The coach picks two captains and says, "Sue, you are one captain and Joe you are the other; pick your team." Everybody gets picked except for Bruce. How does Bruce feel? Terrible...Rip! He's left out. Coach intervenes, "Bruce, you go right here on Joe's team." What do the kids do? "Oh, no! Not him! Now we're really going to lose!" That just ripped another piece out of his sign. Children should not be put into these situations, yet it occurs everywhere—in school classes, in playgrounds, at home, at parties, during sports events, and during after school activities.

Alternatives:

- Put Gummy Bears in a bag and let each child pick one out. Yellow ones go to the left, green ones on the right, etc.

- Break up spaghetti sticks, short ones here, and long ones there.

- Use a deck of playing cards, clubs on one side, hearts on the other.

11. Bringing up embarrassing features:

We may find some things about our children so adorable and funny. It is natural that we want to share these stories with others. However, children may not wish to have them shared. I have experienced parents telling stories about their children with the child standing there begging the parent not to tell the story, yet the parent continues because they think it's funny.

One mother told a story about how her daughter wet her pants in the market. The mom was laughing while telling it and the daughter, 5 years old, was crying asking her to stop. But the mom said, "Don't be silly! It is a cute story." and continued to tell the story in spite of her daughter's protest.

One dad grabbed his 6-year-old son's rolls of fat calling him "fatty". He said, "Let's count those adorable rolls." The boy said, "Dad, stop", but the dad just continued, until finally the boy got so upset he yelled at his dad and called him names. The boy was the one that got punished for his behavior, not the father.

Just imagine if your spouse did something similar to you? I'm betting you would not be happy and would think your feelings were unimportant. Our children deserve the same respect.

12. Yelling:

Why do parents yell? Most of the time it's because they're frustrated with their children.

They have told them ten times to pick up their toys and it hasn't been done. They want them to listen and believe if they say it louder it will be more effective. It's helpful to know that the more you yell the more ineffective you are because yelling becomes your regular tone of voice and eventually means nothing. You may be thinking, "What? No yelling? My whole discipline program is blown. What's left?"

The more you yell, the more you show your children:

- You are out of control

- How to push your buttons,

- If you don't get your way it is OK to be out of control.

We are products of our environment. We learn how to discipline through our parents and so, if we had parents that were "yellers", yelling comes naturally. Many of us believed ourselves to be calm, rational people until we had children. That's when calm went right out the window because children are masterful at pushing our buttons.

> **VOLUME IS NOT CONTROL IF IT SHOWS YOU ARE OUT OF CONTROL**

Keep in mind that volume doesn't mean you are in control; it shows you are out of control.

Please don't misunderstand me. It is unrealistic to think a parent would never lose their temper and yell. We all get frustrated and lose it. It is normal for parents to get angry with their kids. Some self-esteem books have us believing that you must always be happy and positive with your children. Children need to learn that people can be angry and release tension in complete safety. It is equally important for children to see that their behaviors cause reactions. However, like all things, look at the frequency and intensity at which the yelling happens. Do you express your angry feelings without hurting or attacking the person?

My first concern with yelling is that we tend to go into attack mode. We don't just yell about the behavior, we attack the person and we bring up old baggage. "Your room is a mess, you are always such a slob, you will never find a husband once they see what a pig you are. Plus your grades are going down and I don't like those friends you hang out with." And on and on we go. We do it with our spouses as well. "You didn't take the garbage out, and when is the last time you bought me flowers or took me out to dinner?" etc.

My second concern with yelling is, your intended message is not getting across. We may yell because we care about our children and want them to learn right from wrong, but does that message of love get through? I am going to summarize with an example Jane Nelson uses in her book, *Positive Discipline*, which makes an excellent point.

Mrs. Smith, a single parent, called for help with a problem she was having with her fourteen-year-old daughter, Maria. Mrs. Smith was afraid Maria might be getting into drugs. She had found a six-pack of beer on the floor in Maria's closet. When Mrs. Smith confronted Maria about the beer, Maria denied it and the situation escalated into a screaming match.

When Mrs. Smith called Jane for some advice, Jane asked, "Why were you upset about finding the beer?"

She thought that was a stupid question as she indignantly replied, "Because I don't want her to get into trouble."

"Why don't you want her to get into trouble?" was the next question.

Mrs. Smith was sorry she had called as she answered with total irritation, "Because I don't want her to ruin her life!"

Since she still hadn't discovered her bottom-line message,

36

Jane persisted. "And why is it that you don't want her to ruin her life"

She finally got it. "Because I love her!" Mrs. Smith exclaimed.

The final question was asked gently. "Do you think she got that message?"

Mrs. Smith realized she had not come even close to conveying her message of love to Maria.

My third concern with yelling is that it gives children the attention they crave in a negative way because children would rather have negative attention than no attention at all. They would rather have you yelling and screaming at them rather than being ignored.

A story from Steve Biddulph's book "*The Secret of Happy Children*" will explain this clearly.

"Mice and Men"

A few years ago, psychologists wore white coats and worked mostly with rats. (Nowadays they wear tweed jackets and work mostly with young women – things are looking up!) The "rat psychologists" were able to learn a lot about behavior because they could do things with rats that they couldn't with children. Read on, and you'll see what I mean.

In one particular experiment, rats were placed in a special cage, with food and drink, and a little lever. They ate, drank, and ran around, and eventually asked themselves the same question you are asking: "What's the little lever for?" They pressed it (being like children, they wanted to try everything) and, to their surprise, a little window opened in the cage to reveal a film being shown on the wall outside. Perhaps it was "Mickey Mouse" I don't know! The window soon closed and the rat had to press the lever again to get more of the movie.

The rats were willing to work very hard at lever-pressing to keep the movie in view, leading us to principle one: intelligent creatures, such as rats (and children), like to have something interesting to do. This helps their brains to grow.

The researchers then put the rats in a different cage with food and drink but no lever and no window. The rats were content for a little while but then started misbehaving. They chewed the walls, fought with each other, rubbed their fur off, and were generally bad rats. This leads us to principle two: intelligent, creatures, such as rats (and children), will do anything to keep from being bored, including things we could call silly or destructive.

Finally, the researchers really got nasty. They tried a cage with food and drink, and little wires placed across the floor and attached to a battery. Every now and then a shock was sent through the wires, enough to give the little creatures a real start but not to injure them. (You see now why they didn't use children.)

Finally, the exciting moment arrived. The rats were taken out of the cages and given a choice of which cage they would prefer to go back into. Perhaps you, the reader, could make a guess as to which was the rats' first choice, second choice, and so on. Here they are again:

- *Cage with food, drink, and movies*

- *Cage with food and drink*

- *Cage with food, drink, and unexpected shocks*

Have you guessed? Well, the rats preferred the movies best of all. If you didn't guess that one ... back to the start of the book! The second choice was the really interesting one: they preferred the cage with shocks to the one with only food and drink. This leads us to principle three, an important principle indeed for children: intelligent creatures, like rats (and children), would rather have bad things happening than nothing at all.

My fourth concern with yelling is it fills a child's need for power in a negative way. Children have very little power in their lives. Parents dictate what time they should get up, what they should wear to school, what they should take for lunch, what time they have to go to bed and what friends they can have. The only power children have is pushing their buttons. A child would rather see a parent lose control and thus suffer the consequences because it then gives them power. When you lose control, they say to themselves, "There he goes, another temper tantrum. This is better than watching HBO, I've got to remember this technique for tomorrow night." ☺

When you respond by yelling you may be giving your child attention or power but you are ripping both their IALAC sign and yours. After you've finished yelling you most likely feel guilty. "How could I have done this to my child, I must be a bad parent." You may feel so guilty you end up giving in, which sends mixed messages to your child.

©Bill Keane, Inc. Reprinted with Special Permission of King Features Syndicate

Awareness is the first step!

Alternatives to Yelling:

Be proactive: Plan ahead in order to decrease your frustration. It is inevitable that when two or more children go for a car ride an argument will break out and you end up yelling. Knowing this, what is your plan? (Other than, "I am going to pull this car over and you will get out and walk home!")

When a child's friend comes over, you know he will not want to share his new truck. Instead of yelling that he is selfish, what is your plan? When you have a plan you are more likely to respond to the situation rather than react with yelling and threatening.

Pretend you are someone else: Think of someone in your life that is very calm and patient.......... I know, I know, I have no role models to choose from either. So you may want to pick someone from TV or the movies, such as James Bond. (without the weapons!) You become an actor or actress before you walk over to deal with your misbehaving child. Get into character, and begin thinking, " Bond, James Bond". Remain calm and cool just as he would when dealing with your child.

There is a saying "FAKE IT TILL YOU MAKE IT". If you pretend to be a calm and in-control parent long enough, eventually you will become calm. (Too bad it doesn't work for all things folks!I've been pretending to be thin for ages, and it still hasn't worked!! ☺)

The idea is when you respond a few times in a calm fashion, and you see the positive results, it will reinforce the calm behavior.

Be brief: If you want to be heard use one word or one sentence, and talk less. When you talk in paragraphs, kids stop listening after the first sentence.

Parents may say, "You have to brush your teeth. If you don't brush your teeth they are going to rot, then they'll fall out and then you are going to need dentures like grandpa." and on and on and on.

How about "Tommy, teeth. "He'll know what you mean.

OR

"I've been asking and asking you kids to get in your pajamas

40

all night and all you have been doing is clowning around. I agreed to let you watch TV before you got into your pajamas, but I certainly don't see any one of you holding up your end of the bargain. I can't trust you to do what you promise. No more TV." Try: "Kids, pajamas."

OR

"You forgot your book bag. You would forget your head if it wasn't attached." Instead "Jamie, your book bag."

That's all. It's that simple. Again, it's hard because we are in the habit of going on and on and on.

The funny thing is that children only listen to the first few words that come out of your mouth; they tune the rest out. They think, "Oh here comes lecture 212--heard it a thousand times", then they click off. After the first few words all they hear is Charlie Brown's teacher saying "wah wah wah wah wah." Then children stop listening and then their minds tune you out and then you're words fall on deaf ears, and then all the breath you are using is being wasted and then at the end of the day you're exhausted from talking so much and then your spouse comes home and you are short tempered with him and then you have a big fight and go to bed crying. ☺ **GET IT?**

Make your message clear in the first line even though you may have to repeat those couple of words two or three times before they actually obey.

If you did more of this you wouldn't be as exhausted at the end of the day. You might even have enough energy to have another child. ☺

Emotions Are Contagious—You Get What You Give

The world is a reflection of ourselves.
When we hate ourselves,
we hate everybody else.

3

☺ ☺ ☺

CHARACTERISTICS OF BOTH A HEALTHY AND UNHEALTHY SELF-ESTEEM

Feelings of inferiority and superiority are the same.
They both come from fear.

In order to help you better identify if you or your child need to work on areas of self-esteem, look at the lists below.

Be aware that the list is not foolproof. Some things may be developmental or occur during a time of crisis. It is important when looking at the list to look at the duration and frequency of the behavior.

Characteristics Of An Unhealthy Self-Esteem

Children and adults with low self-esteem tend to:

1. Avoid situations where failure is feared

2. Lack commitment

3. Avoid eye contact

4. Brag

5. Speak negatively about themselves and their achievements

6. Be easily influenced by others

7. Value others' opinions over their own

8. Try to please people

9. Complain

10. Be unable to accept compliments

11. Get frustrated easily

12. Often feel jealous or guilty

13. Say "yes" when they want to say "no"

14. Make excuses for their shortcomings and do not accept responsibility for their actions

15. Be perfectionists

16. Have difficulty accepting any type of criticism

17. Act superior and put down others

18. Exaggerate or lie to maintain an image

19. Command situations in an aggressive/critical manner

20. Have the need to justify/rationalize mistakes

21. Procrastinate

22. Be materialistic

23. Be angry often and hold grudges

24. Be overwhelmed with life

25. Put self down constantly

Characteristics Of A Healthy Self-Esteem

Children and adults with high self-esteem tend to:

1. Have high energy levels

2. Take care of themselves (physically and emotionally)

3. Have a positive/optimistic attitude

4. Maintain eye contact

5. Take responsibility for their actions

6. Make their own choices and decisions

7. Have the ability to accept and give compliments

8. Welcome new challenges

9. Appreciate others' achievements as well as their own

10. Set goals for themselves and reach them

11. Look at problems as potential opportunities to learn and grow

12. Trust others

13. Feel free to express their own opinions (and can say "no")

14. Have the ability to laugh at themselves, without degrading themselves

15. Push themselves to expand their comfort zones

16. Try again, if they fail at a task

17. Be free from guilt and jealousy

18. Enjoy being by themselves

19. Make friends easily

20. Not be judgmental

21. Apologize for mistakes

22. Use positive self-talk

23. Display good sportsmanship

24. Be willing to hear others' opinions

25. Forgive others and not hold grudges

Check Your Self-Esteem

Barksdale Self-Esteem Evaluation No. 69

(This is an EVALUATION, not a test)

This Self-Esteem Evaluation measures your current level of self-esteem, your Self-Esteem Index (SEI), and serves as a gauge of your progress in achieving sound self-esteem. It is important to clearly understand all statements and be completely honest in your scoring if you are to obtain a valid SEI. It is essential that you answer these statements according to how you actually feel or behave, instead of how you think you "should" feel or behave.

Score as follows (each score shows how true or the amount of time you believe that statement is true for you):

0 = not at all true for me

1 = somewhat true or true only part of the time

2 = fairly true or true about half the time

3 = mainly true or true most of the time

4 = true all the time

Scoring = 0 1 2 3 4

Self-Esteem Statements

_____ **1.** I don't feel anyone else is better than I am.

_____ **2.** I am free of shame, blame, and guilt.

_____ **3.** I am a happy, carefree person.

_____ **4.** I have no need to prove I am as good as or better than others.

_____ **5.** I do not have a strong need for people to pay attention to me or like what I do.

_____ **6.** Losing does not upset me or make me feel "less than" others.

_____ **7.** I feel warm and loving toward myself.

_____ **8.** I do not feel others are better than I am because they can do things better, have more money, or are more popular.

_____ **9.** I am at ease with strangers and make friends easily.

_____ **10.** I speak up for my own ideas, likes, and dislikes.

_____ **11.** I am not hurt by others' opinions or attitude.

_____ **12.** I do not need praise to feel good about myself.

_____ **13.** I feel good about others' good luck and winning.

_____ **14.** I do not find fault with my family, friends, or others.

_____ **15.** I do not feel I must always please others.

_____ **16.** I am open and honest, and not afraid of letting people see my real self.

_____ **17.** I am friendly, thoughtful, and generous toward others.

_____ **18.** I do not blame others for my problems and mistakes.

_____ **19.** I enjoy being alone with myself.

_____ **20.** I accept compliments and gifts without feeling uncomfortable or needing to give something in return.

_____ **21.** I admit my mistakes and defeats without feeling ashamed or "less than."

_____ **22.** I feel no need to defend what I think, say, or do.

_____ **23.** I do not need others to agree with me or tell me I'm right.

_____ **24.** I do not brag about myself, what I have done, or what my family has or does.

_____ **25.** I do not feel "put down" when criticized by my friends or others.

The possible range of your Self-Esteem Index is from 0 to 100. Sound self-esteem is indicated by an SEI of 95 or more. Good self-esteem is indicated by a score of 90 to 94. Experience shows that any score under 90 is a disadvantage, a score of 75 or less is a serious handicap, and an SEI of 50 or less indicates a really crippling lack of self-esteem.

Self-Esteem Questionnaire For Working Adults

Mark a T (true) or an F (false) for each statement as it normally relates to your thinking.

_____ **1.** I feel my work/career has progressed more because of luck than because I deserve it.

_____ **2.** I often find myself thinking, "Why can't I be more successful?"

_____ **3.** I do not believe I am working to my potential.

_____ **4.** I consider it a failure when I do not accomplish my goals.

_____ **5.** When others are nice to me, I often feel suspicious.

_____ **6.** Giving others compliments about their strengths often makes me feel uncomfortable.

_____ **7.** It is difficult to see co-workers promoted because I often feel I am more deserving.

_____ **8.** I do not necessarily believe that our minds have a direct influence on our physical well being.

_____ **9.** When things are going well, it usually will not last for me.

_____ **10.** I place a high value on what others think of me.

_____ **11.** I like to impress my supervisor.

_____ **12.** I find it difficult to face up to my mistakes.

_____ **13.** I am not always comfortable saying what I mean.

_____ **14.** I find it hard to say, "I am sorry."

_____ **15.** I tend to accept change in my job slowly because of fear.

_____ **16.** Procrastination is a good word to describe my work habits.

_____ **17.** I often find myself thinking, "Why even try? I won't make it."

_____ **18.** When my boss praises me, I usually do not believe him or her.

_____ **19.** I think my co-workers do not want me to advance professionally.

_____ **20.** I avoid people who I think do not like me.

_____ **21.** My attitude toward life could improve.

_____ **22.** I tend to blame my parents for how my life is turning out.

_____ **23.** I find it difficult to look for the good in others.

_____ **24.** I do not think people can change their attitudes.

_____ **25.** I really do not believe that a self-help book will make a difference in one's self-esteem.

Add up all your TRUE and FALSE statements.

If you scored over half of the items TRUE, you may want to spend some quality time with yourself, or with a counselor, thinking about your life. Think about why you have these feelings. If the majority of your answers were FALSE, you seem to have good self-esteem and are on your way to greater success and satisfaction.

Attitude is the key and
Inner Success is the first step to Outer Success

4

☺ ☺ ☺

THE GIFT OF UNCONDITIONAL LOVE

I am happy simply because you exist!

Unconditional love is accepting and loving another without any restrictions; loving another with all of their flaws and shortcomings. "Love me for me, not for what I do or achieve."

Conditional love says, "If you do what I want you to do, the way I want you to do it, then I will love you."

Every human being seeks unconditional love. In fact, that is usually what we are looking for in the mate we choose to marry, one who will love us when we are old, fat, bald, have bad breath, and make mistakes. Even though we, ourselves, so desperately seek unconditional love we rarely give this gift to others, not even to our children. Parents get upset when a child does not live up to their expectations and they withdraw their approval or love to let the child know, "You let me down".

Children learn at an early age that love is conditional. "I will only be loved if I am good, if I have a clean room, get good grades." Conditional love is learned at a young age through parents' daily actions, words and tone of voice. For example:

The child will not share a toy with a visiting friend.
Parent response "You are so selfish. Go to your room."

The child spills his soda on the floor.
Parent response, "You never listen. I told you to slow down, now get out of here!"

The child gets a poor report card.
Parent response, "I am so disappointed in you, why can't you study like your brother?"

Your child gets into a fight with another sibling and comes to you complaining.
Parent response, "I've had enough of you, just go outside and get away from me."

What a child assumes from the above examples is that when he does something wrong or makes a mistake, his parents get angry, they don't want to be near him and they don't love him.

Please realize that a few of these occurrences will not have any real harmful effect on a child, but over the years they accumulate and the child learns that to be approved and to be loved, he has to be perfect. He can't make mistakes.

Perfectionists constantly seek approval. What others think becomes their motivation and they pour all of their energy

> SOMETIMES, OUT OF CONDITIONAL LOVE A PERFECTIONIST CHILD IS CREATED

into becoming what they think others want them to be. They always try to measure up to unreachable standards.

Learn to separate the doer from the deed. "I love you, but I don't like your behavior." Naturally this is much easier said than done. It is very hard to do when you are angry or upset, which is why it is often best to wait until you are calm before discussing concerns with your child. "I am angry that you didn't listen to me and now my dish is broken; we will both take a time out and talk when we are calm."

Often parents complain that when their child reaches adolescence they don't talk, share their feelings, or share what is going on in their life. Part of this is the normal stage of a child becoming independent and the other part may be that the child grew up in a home where love was conditional. When the child shared how they didn't do their homework, failed a test, or was sent to the principal's office and was responded to with yelling, blaming, and punishing, it naturally follows that their thinking will progress to, "It is better to not to tell my parents anything."

In counseling, before an adolescent shares some "secret" the most common responses heard are, "I'll tell you but you must promise you won't tell my mom? Whatever you do don't tell my parents, because they will hate me, they'll kill me, they'll kick me out, or they'll never talk to me." Then they divulge things, such as: "I am failing all my classes, I had sex, I do drugs, I'm pregnant, or, I wish I were dead."

As a parent we want to be the person our child comes to in the time of a crisis, in their time of need, yet we are the last person they turn to. Why? Because they believe our love is conditional. They've learned that for approval and love, they have to be good and not make mistakes. Please don't misunderstand my point. As a parent it is natural to be upset and you have every right to be upset. It is also appropriate to provide consequences if your child told you any of the above things. "I'm upset that you're pregnant. There are going to be consequences, (you are never going out again until you are 55. ☺) But you know I love you and somehow we will get through this together." Of course you may not be able to say this until the initial shock wears off! The key is separating the doer from the deed.

Parents often say, "I always tell my children that they can come and tell me anything no matter what it is...I will always be here for them." Well that's nice to say, but your daily actions speak louder than your words.

Let's pretend you had a car accident and smashed the family car. Whether or not you tell your spouse right away, or you tell them the whole truth all depends on their reaction to past mistakes or accidents. When you tell them about the accident, which response makes you feel you are unconditionally loved?

A) Lectures you on being more careful.

B) Carries on about how careless you are and how expensive it is going to be to repair the car.

C) Says that the important thing is you are not hurt and together you will figure out a way to pay for the deductible portion of the insurance.

The following are suggestions on ways to provide unconditional love:

1. Give A Hug
"Emotional CPR": one hug, one deep breath. Repeat.

The recommended daily requirement for hugs is:

- Four per day for survival

- Eight per day for maintenance

- Twelve per day for growth.

Touch is vital to life. It is the first sense to develop. It is an extremely critical element for human development. We need to be caressed, and cuddled as much as we need food. If babies do not get touched frequently, nerve endings send fewer signals to the brain. Most of the neuro-chemical changes in the brain occur as a result of direct tactile stimulation. Babies that do not get enough touch suffer "failure to thrive syndrome" and, in extreme cases, studies have shown that babies who are deprived of touch can actually die. We learned about touch from our parents. If they cuddled and hugged us often, we learned to enjoy touch. If they didn't touch us at all, we learned either to crave physical contact or to physically close ourselves off to others. Younger children are more likely to get hugs than older children. The smaller or cuter they are, the more affection they get. The older or more defiant they are the fewer hugs they tend to get. Yet that is when they need it the most.

When an infant is first born he receives a great deal of

physical touching; this declines a little when breast-feeding ends and bottle-feeding begins. It again decreases when another sibling is born into the family. It declines again when a child becomes a teenager. The way teenagers get more physical touch is to get a boyfriend or girlfriend, or have a child of their own to hug and touch. Some teenagers may not be open to a good old bear hug, so find other ways to touch (Dance, wrestle, touch their arm while talking).

A hug validates a child's existence. Hugs sometimes say things better than words.

Hugs are a quick easy way to say:

I care.

I notice.

I love you.

I value you.

You're special.

I appreciate you.

I need you.

You are adorable.

You bring joy to my life.

You're the best.

You messed up, but I still love you.

This is a difficult situation to be in; I will be here to support you.

I don't know what to say to help you feel better, let me give you a hug just to let you know I care and I am here for you.

I mentioned before that one reason children tend to misbehave is to gain attention, because negative attention is

better than no attention at all. A
hug is one way to give
attention in a positive way
rather than a negative way.

Parents are not mind readers.
They do not always know that
a child might need or want
attention and many children do
not know how to ask for it. I
found that starting with a more
concrete request makes it
easier for children to make
adults aware of their needs. The
concrete method I have used to teach
children to request attention is the
"Hug coupon",

"Sometimes when you hurt
inside, no medicine can
fix it. Only a hug can."

©Bill Keane, Inc. Reprinted with
Special Permission of
King Features Syndicate

or for older children, "Attention Please" coupons.

One of the things I do in my classroom is use "hug
coupons". When a child needs attention and I'm not aware
of it, instead of throwing a
chair in frustration, a child
can go to my desk and get a
hug coupon and give it to
me. That is a way of telling
me he needs some type of
attention. If I were to give

you a hug coupon, that would be my way of letting you
know that I care about you. You can keep the hug coupon or
you can pass it on to someone else and give him or her a
hug. I first started this with eleven and twelve year old boys

56

in a class of emotionally handicapped children. When I told them about it, some laughed, some were happy, some rolled their eyes. I started by just giving them out at random times. Then one by one they started coming and giving them to me in exchange for a hug. They were comfortable giving them to me to get a hug, but not to each other. I told them they could pass it on to their classmates if they saw someone who needed attention or someone who was feeling down as a way to cheer them up. Their response was, "No way!" It took one brave boy, Ron, who gave a hug coupon along with a hug to another student. After a while, it became accepted in our class and we didn't even need the hug coupons. Everyone got a hug when they were happy, a hug when they needed encouragement, a hug when they came into the room, when they left at the end of the day, when they failed a test and when they passed a test.

In February, a new 11-year-old boy named John came into my class and observed all of this hugging going on. He walked up to me and whispered, "Are you guys queer in here or something?" This was his introduction to Special Education. I said, "No, John. We give hugs when we want to let someone know that we care, and that they are not alone. You know, how your mom and dad hug you before you go to bed at night?"

"My mom and dad don't hug me," John said.

"Before they send you off to school they might give you a hug or a kiss?"

"My mom and dad don't hug and kiss me!"

He was eleven years old. He didn't even know what a hug was. He wasn't comfortable with giving or getting a hug and I never force hugs on someone who is not a hugger. I said, "John, if you're not comfortable giving a hug, that's okay. When you give me a hug coupon, I'll just give you a pat on the back. That will be your way of knowing that I care about you." That worked well for a couple of months. Then one day John approached me and said, "Mrs. B, look! I got an A!" I replied, "Good job!" and gave him a pat on the back. He responded, "But it was an A." That was my cue to give him a hug. Soon after that he would come up and give me a hug coupon. I would hug him; however, he didn't hug back. It took a year and a half before John could come and get or give a hug without a reason why. People say he was not a hugger, maybe because he never had one. Maybe because he didn't feel he was worthy of one.

Hugs also diffuse anger as shown in this comic strip.

When I was teaching four, five, and six year olds, there was a boy in my class named Mike. Mike was the bully of the class and the kids learned not to go near Mike when he was having a bad day. Jason had seen that Mike was in a bad mood and he walked up to my desk, picked up a hug coupon, and started heading towards Mike. I was beginning to get nervous regarding Jason's safety. He was very smart, though. He placed the hug coupon on Mike's desk, walked behind Mike's chair and hugged Mike from behind. Mike's face just melted. The anger just drained away. Mike sat there for ten minutes, then got up and passed the hug coupon on to someone else, and then it went to someone else, and to someone else. Ahh, the power of a hug!

Hugs are ways of showing children that you love them no matter what. It's a way for them to get the attention they need. With some children, we don't realize how much attention they actually need. **WARNING:** 4 and 5-year-olds love hug coupons. It may reach a point where you have to say, "Put the hug coupon away and get to bed!"

2. Telling Your Child "I Love You."

Children and adults love to hear these three very important words.

People say, "My child knows I love them. I feed them. I clothe them. I put up with them, don't I? Of course I love them." While it's wonderful that your actions show your love, it is also important to hear it.

A friend of mine has been married for 25 years. Only once has she ever heard her husband say, "I love you." You can tell they love each other. They are very affectionate and loving but he can't say those three little words that mean so much. Even though she feels his love, she longs to hear it. His parents never spoke those words to him and the unfortunate result is that his children are being deprived of hearing those precious words, and their children in turn may never hear those words. Things tend to pass down from generation to generation. Hopefully someone, whether it is my friend or one of her children, will break the cycle. Learned behavior is quite difficult to change; if you are one who finds it difficult to say "I love you", try putting it in a note and sticking it in a lunch bag, a shirt or sweater pocket or leaving a message on an answering machine or sending it in an e-mail. It is important and I would encourage you to find a way to say these three words to those you love.

The one regret people often have after a tragedy such as the World Trade Center is, "I didn't get a chance to tell them how much I love them." Why aren't we telling them everyday when they wake up and every night when they go to bed? Let people know how much you love them. Children and adults can never hear these words enough

It is not "I love you" because you clean your room, or do the dishes, or stay out of trouble, it's "I love you" because you are you. I will still love you even when you make mistakes and drive me crazy.

3. Using Descriptive Praise

Families remind each other of their goodness:
Unhealthy families remind each other of their failings."
-Matthew Fox

The people we love and care about the most are often the people we praise the least. We tend to take them for granted. We begin to expect rather than appreciate. Perhaps it's your job to take care of the lawn and someone says, "Wow, the lawn looks so thick and green!" After you pick yourself up from the floor from shock that someone noticed, ☺ you would most likely begin to feel appreciated, and taking care of the lawn would no longer be such drudgery.

Children need compliments too. It is your children's job to do their homework. Why not make their day by saying, "I've noticed all month you've been working hard at getting your homework done on time with very few mistakes". The more positive attention you give the less negative attention they demand.

Often when people hear the word "praise" they think it means gratuitous praise. While "generic praise", expressions like, "Oh, you're wonderful! You're so smart! You are terrific! You're super! It's beautiful!" can be very uplifting, they can also be very harmful.

Okay, I know what you're thinking, "Great. Now I don't even praise correctly, what next?" ☺

Praise can be a magic wand or it can be a weapon. Given correctly it can help a child feel capable and secure; given incorrectly it can cause insecurity and anxiety.

Let's look at reasons why generic praise is not helpful.

A. The child often may be unsure of what they did that you like so much.

"That was terrific!" "What was so terrific? When I kicked Tommy under the table, is that what was so great"?

Children need to know the exact behavior for which they're being complimented. In this way, they begin to feel good about themselves and have the desire to succeed.

B. Generic praise uses evaluating words such as:

Good, great, wonderful, fantastic and super. Imagine that a friend says to you, "You look fantastic today!" and the next day the same friend says, "You look nice today." Exactly what did you do to go down a notch from fantastic to nice? You don't have a clue, but you know you don't look as good!

Good, great, wonderful, fantastic and super evaluate the child's character rather than their efforts, progress or achievement. While these praises make a child feel good for the moment, it may also say to him that he is good only because.......and then you have the beginnings of a "people pleaser". It is much more effective to say, "That was a great essay because you put all the sentences in the right paragraphs, your punctuation was correct and your subject was well researched. You're right on target."

Evaluating words also tend to be unrealistic and can give a child a false sense of confidence, such as: "I'm the greatest because that is what my parents always tell me."

C. Generic praise is unrealistic and difficult to live up to.

"You got all A's. You're the smartest girl!" The child may translate this to mean, "If I don't get A's, I am not smart."

"You are my shining star; I can always count on you to do the right thing."

Translation: "If I make a mistake, you won't love me."

"What a good girl you are; you ate all your dinner."

Translation: "If I am not hungry and don't eat dinner, I am not a good girl?"

D. When we use generic praise with evaluating words it tends to be extravagant and may sound dishonest.

Extravagant praise can make a child question its sincerity. Sometimes the more extravagantly we praise, the less it gets through, the praise loses its value and means nothing to the child.

Adult: "What an absolutely terrific poem you wrote! Why it's stupendous. I can't get over how great it is."
Child's thought: "She really doesn't mean it."

"I am very moved by your poem about the sunset. I especially enjoyed the line about..." would be more believable and encouraging to a child because it shows you actually took the time to read the poem.

Try saying, "You have picked up all your toys and made your bed. Thanks, I appreciate your help." Instead of, "Your room looks terrific, what a good cleaner you are."

Praise needs to be honest; it should not be a lie. Describe what you see. Try to avoid saying things you don't believe. If a child shows you a picture and you have no idea what it is, rather than say, "Oh what a beautiful picture!" describe what you are seeing. "From the expression on your face it looks like you are very proud of your picture." Or, "I see you used many bright colors in your picture." Or "Tell me about your picture"

Praise needs to be very specific, describe exactly what it is the child did.

"You came to the dinner table the first time I called you, thanks."

"Thank you for folding the clothes; it was big help."

"I appreciate that you picked up your toys right after you were done playing."

Use a word to sum up the child's praise-worthy behavior.

"Thank you for calling to say you would be late. That was very responsible of you."

"I notice you shared your snack with your younger brother. That was generous."

"I appreciate your cleaning the kitchen when I was sick; it was really thoughtful of you."

This type of praise tells them exactly what they did and gives them a positive label to live up to.

"I like the way you are helping your sister clean."

Starting praise with the words 'I like' is something we were taught in school or learned from our parents. It is not helpful. It shows that your love is conditional. You only like me when I do good things. It says:

I should do things just because you like it, just to please you, not because it is the right thing to do.

My concern is that using the words "I like" will create a generation of "praise junkies". Children will become dependent on outside approval. Subsequently, as they grow older they will become more susceptible to peer pressure having learned from early childhood to do things to please others, not because it is the right thing to do.

The above suggestions regarding praise do one very important thing: they teach children how to assess themselves realistically. Adolescents are not exempt from needing specific praise. They, too need to know they are appreciated even though they are not about to admit it. We're never too old to receive praise. Do you enjoy receiving praise? I'm sure you do, and look at how old you are! We don't give enough of it. I am amazed, because when

I counsel, parents say things like, "I think I might be praising my child too much." Yet I never hear them say "I think I might be criticizing my child too much." If you are giving a lot of empty praise then, yes, you are giving too much false confidence and comments like this are not heard as sincere. They don't mean anything. When praise is sincere and specific you can never give too much.

It only takes a few kind words to make you feel valued and loved.

4. Writing Notes

Another way to give specific praise and unconditional love is by writing notes. I am a big believer in writing notes. When you write a note it means you took the time to find paper, a pencil and to think of something and write it down. Now, I have that note to keep forever to remind me on the days I am feeling down that someone cares.

It doesn't really matter whether you use a Post-it® note, a store bought or handmade card, or a piece of scrap paper. Just write a sincere and specific comment to your child, spouse, friend, sibling or parent.

Put a note in their lunch bag, book bag, leave it on their pillow, on the mirror, on the steering wheel in the car, or write it on the next page in their math notebook. And, remember try not to leave these notes only when your child does something good, but also leave them when they need a reminder that you love them, when you need to apologize, when they need encouragement, when they are having a bad day, when they put in effort and don't have the expected success.

One father used what he calls "Post-it® Therapy. He would write little sticky notes and leave them for his daughter. She saved them and put them on the back of her bedroom door. She is now an adolescent, and the door is almost completely covered. When she goes in her room and slams the door and says, "Everybody hates me" there on the back of her door is a reminder of how much she is loved.

I once counseled a sixteen-year-old girl, named Tina. Tina was a real hard-nosed, snot-faced, unlikable child. How is that for positive...? ☺ I was having a hard time reaching her. I said to the mother, "She needs to know that you care about her. She needs to know that you love her." The mother's response was, "What? Are you kidding me? Tina could care less whether I love her or not and to be honest with you, there are days that I don't feel a lot of love towards her." (Those of you who have teenagers can relate to that comment because there may have been days when you wonder why you ever wanted children? ☺) I requested that she make an effort and write Tina a positive note that conveyed care and concern. She left Tina a note on her pillow that simply said, "Hope you had a nice day. Love, Mom." When Tina read it, she looked at her mom, crumbled it up and threw it on the floor.

If you put your heart on your sleeve and someone stabs it, what would your reaction be? "I'll never do that again. That was a stupid idea." That was exactly what her mother said when she called me. "That was so stupid. It didn't work. I told you she doesn't care if I love her. It means nothing to her." She was very upset. This is understandable. In our society if we don't receive a quick and positive response to something new, we give up.

A similar example is when I go on a diet. If I don't lose 30 pounds in three days, it's the stupidest diet and I give up. Why? Because for three days I deprived myself of something I enjoy. I made myself do things that I don't enjoy (like eating vegetables) so I want some quick results. I have to realize that it didn't take me three days to put on 30 pounds and it will take more than three days to lose it.

Getting back to Tina. She built up a wall of anger and hate over 16 years and one note could not possibly make that wall come crashing down She was nowhere near ready to open up and be vulnerable to being hurt. I asked the mother to leave her a note everyday. The mom left her a note on her pillow, on her blow dryer, on the mirror; anywhere that Tina would see it when she came home from school. At the end of only one week the mother called me and said, "You're not going to believe it. Tina came in the house, threw down her books and ran around to see where I left the note today." It's amazing to think that even a hard-nosed, snot-faced 16-year-old could care about a note. It is another way of letting someone know you care. Please don't misunderstand me; Tina was not a perfect angel after one week of notes. It took a lot of counseling and time to make changes, but gradually there were changes in her behavior.

I tell Tina's story to demonstrate that even the most difficult children will respond if we, as adults, are persistent in our attempt to show them unconditional love.

CAUTION: Sarcastic notes are poison:

"Yeah, you did it...you finally took the garbage out!

"WOW there is a floor in your bedroom!"

This is negative humor and does not express appreciation.

Making a request for your child to do chores is another way to use note writing.

I'm sure most of us have had a note like this left for us at one time or another. "This kitchen better be clean by the time I get home!"

Wouldn't it have been better to read, "I look forward to coming home to a clean kitchen."

My husband listens to many of my workshops and one day I received a note from him. It said "Things for the most beautiful woman in the world to do today" and he left a list of things and signed it "I love you." You better believe that I did every one of those things! ☺

The wonderful thing about notes is that you have no idea of the lasting effect that note will have or how much it will mean later on. They may keep the note to reread because it gives them a needed lift to get through a difficult day. Think about a time that you might have received a note from a teacher or from a parent and it meant so much to you that you saved it.

At one time, my father was going through a job change and I felt really bad for him. He was really depressed and I didn't know what to say. Very often when we are uncomfortable with what to say, we say nothing. So writing a note is sometimes easier. I wrote little notes and drew pictures on them and put them on the mirror where my father shaved every morning. He said if it weren't for those notes, he wouldn't have gotten up everyday. He got up each day just to see what the note would say. Those notes meant so much to him that he went as far as to frame them and they hung in the bathroom for years. Had I known that I would have done better artwork! ☺

It doesn't take long to write a few loving words on a piece of paper so why not try it.

5. Creating A Feeling Of Importance

Please answer these two questions.

What is most important in your life?

What do you spend most of your time on?

Did the answers to question one and two match? Do you spend most of your time with what you listed as important to you? Most people list family as most important but list work as where they spend most of their time. We spend most of our time on what we value, on what is important to us. If you are not spending a lot of time with your children they logically conclude, "I am not that important." Want to make your child feel loved and feel important? Spend time with them.

Children spell love "T-I-M-E".

Many times I've heard:

"Daddy will you play with me?"

"No honey, I don't have time right now."

"Mommy will you play with me?"

"I am too busy to play right now."

I often hear parents say, "Well I work many hours to provide for my family so that they can have the finer things in life." Great, so your children live in a big house, have nice clothes and a fancy car, but they live with strangers who give them lots of "presents," but not their "presence."

When you don't have time for your child the message is clear, "I am not a priority". You have no time to read a story, to play ball, to color with them, build a Lego city, sing songs, or play at the park. Yet you have time for your job, for your friends, to clean the house, to work on the lawn or the computer. When you have time for everything and everyone else except your child, they begin to feel that they are unimportant to you. They feel as if they aren't worth your time or your energy and that hurts no matter who you are or how old you are. Think of yourself and your spouse. When your spouse is so busy with other things, don't you feel neglected, hurt and unimportant? Children feel the same way.

If you are having quantity time that is filled with anger, yelling, or put-downs, then quantity time is counterproductive.

"Quality time" and "quantity time" are two very different concepts.

"Quality time" is having time alone with an individual. It is time where you give your undivided attention to one person, doing things you both enjoy. It's creating memories. Quality time is a wonderful gift. It becomes the time children cherish (especially when a new baby comes into the house) but this does not replace quantity time.

"Quantity time" is being there often. That means often enough to notice that your child is in a good mood, sad or excited, often enough to know what they enjoy or don't enjoy, often enough to know their favorite foods and television shows, their fears, strengths and who their friends are.

I have a concern with the concept of "quality time" or rather the way it is being used today. In our busy lives we justify our lack of quantity time with our children. Quality time is often misused, thinking that it is all right if I don't spend the whole day with my child as long as I get in five minutes of quality time at the end of the day. "Okay honey, I have five minutes. what do you want to talk about?" "What? Now I'm supposed to open up my heart and tell you everything, because you have five minutes to listen to me. Where were you when my best friend and I had a fight? How come you weren't at the soccer game? Where were you during the school play? Where were you when I came home crying because the kids teased me? Where were you when I got the award at school?

Out of the quantity time you get quality moments. Moments where your child will trust you enough and feel close enough to you to open up and tell you how they feel, to tell you what happened in school, and how they felt when the kids made fun of them or when the kids offered them drugs. These types of conversations will rarely occur if you're not there often enough.

6. Showing Interest In What Your Child Is Doing

If your child is involved in some type of a sporting activity, in the debate club or the choir, take the time to go, watch, and listen. Children love it when you show up and you are in the audience clapping and taking pictures of them. Teenagers want you there too. They just don't want you in the back saying "Oh, that's my boy Johnny. Go Johnny Go!" They'll be embarrassed and beg you not to come. I realize that in today's society we have very hectic work schedules and trying to make it to all of your child's after school activities or sporting events may be difficult. I suggest that if you cannot make it to your child's game, go to a practice. It's a great way of saying, "I don't care whether you win or lose, I just want to watch you." This is also very helpful for children with low self-esteem because they may feel too much pressure to impress you by winning when you show up at their games.

When I was growing up I was on the swim team. I was a good back stroker and would often win at the meets. My father would say, "Do you want me to go to the game? I can try to get off early and see if I can go." I would say "No. No. Don't bother." I had a low self-esteem and I figured what if I don't win that one time that he came. It would have been a waste of his time and he might be disappointed in me. Yet, everyday I would wait for my father to walk through the door and he never did because I told him not to. My point is, don't always believe what they are saying, just be there even if you're not invited and be that silent support.

Single parents are doing all they can to take care of the family and hold down a job therefore, it may be impossible to attend your child's events. In this case let them know how much you wish you could be there and have someone video tape parts of the activity. Sit down with your child later to watch it together. If there is no videotape then sit with your child while they tell you all the details of the events.

7. Play "A Star for the Evening"

Each family member is assigned a day of the week. When sitting around the dinner table the child or parent is given the opportunity to be bombarded with positive comments for five minutes.

8. Play "Secret Friends"

Secret Friends is a way to get family members to be more positive and kind to each other. Everyone in the family, including the parents, will put their name in a hat. Each family member takes out one name. (If you pick your own put it back and pick again) You are not allowed to tell whose name you picked. All day long do helpful things and say kind words, not only to your secret friend but to other members of the family. Before bedtime family members try to guess who their secret friend was. Whoever guesses correctly wins. The idea is to do so many kind deeds for everyone so that your secret friend cannot guess who you are.

9. Play Together

Have fun with your children. Be silly, tickle them, wrestle with them, get down on the floor and play with them.

10. Laugh More

Lighten up. The average child laughs 500 times a day. The average adult laughs 15 times a day. BIG difference. When you are laughing you start feeling positive. The more you laugh the better you feel.

11. Build a Warm Fuzzy File

A Warm Fuzzy File is a file folder that has all of the positive things that your child has done, said or achieved. When you get positive notes from the child's teachers, it goes in the file. If they were written up in the school or local paper, it goes in the file. If they received a nice note from a friend, it goes in the file. Good report cards, high test grades, and positive observations that you made, all go into the warm fuzzy file. When a child feels down or defeated he can take out the file and look through the positive things that have happened to him.

When a child says, "Oh, I'm never going to be able to memorize my multiplication facts," Take out their past work, such as addition with regrouping, that they never thought they would be able to do. Take out their old spelling test with a high grade, words that they once said they weren't going to be able to do. The file is there to look at on those days when they think they can't achieve anything. It is showing them their past successes and letting them know there is a chance they can have another success if they keep trying.

One reason I started using the warm fuzzy file with my students is because I recalled when I was a freshman in college, I was having a hard time and didn't think I was going to succeed. I called my father saying, "I have too many classes, I'm not going to be able to do this. I just think I should drop out of school" My father took me through a verbal Warm Fuzzy File. He said "Remember when you were in high school and you didn't think you could do the social studies report; you worked every night on it and you passed? Remember when you were on the track team and you didn't think you could beat your own time but you did!" On and on he went. I was fortunate that my father had such a good memory and could rattle off all these past success, that in my negative state of mind, I would not have remembered. When I hung up the phone I was thinking, "Oh man! I could be president of the United States if I want to!" ☺ I felt so positive because I had achieved all these things. My inner critical voice wouldn't dare let me remember them. I was lucky I had a father who did. Instead of relying on your memories when successes happen, write them down. Even better have your child write them down. Put them in his or her file so that when they need a pick me up it's right there.

Parents also need a Warm Fuzzy File. Unfortunately for you parents, people don't often take the time to recognize or tell you the positive things you do. However, you can do it for yourself. When your boss praises you for handling an account well, write it down. If you made it for a half hour without criticizing or yelling at your children during dinnertime, write it down. Write all your successes on a piece of paper and put them in your own Warm Fuzzy File. This way when you get down on yourself, you have plenty of reminders that you really aren't all that bad. ☺

Kind words can be short and easy to speak,
but their echoes are truly endless.

$$$$$$$$$$$$$$

YOU CAN
ALWAYS
MAKE
MORE MONEY

BUT

YOU CAN
NEVER MAKE
MORE TIME

$$$$$$$$$$$$$$

5

☺ ☺ ☺

INFLUENTIAL ROLE MODELS
IN A CHILD'S LIFE

*It is easier to say what we believe
than be what we believe*

Before you begin reading this chapter please get paper and
pen and write your answers to the following four questions.

**1. What kind of person do you want your child to
become?** (Meaning what values do you want them to have?)

Example: Courage, honesty, ambition, generosity, education,
kindness

**2 What is your plan on how to teach and model these
values?**

3. Would you build a house without blueprints?

**4. Would you plan a dinner party for 20 people without
a menu?**

The answers to number 3 and 4 are usually, NO. Yet, few of
us have ever thought about or written down the answer to
numbers one and two. We seldom plan what we want our
children to become. If we don't take the time to plan we just
continue to play the old tapes from our childhood.

Values help determine your behavior and children learn
values from your behavior and examples. When you take
the time to think and plan what you value and what you
want your child to become, you can then shape your
behavior to promote those values.

How often do you use your good china for a regular family
dinner or buy special food to make an extravagant meal for

your family. Usually these are reserved for guests. Doesn't that tell your family that you value friends or relatives over them?

Let's say you're shopping and you are in a hurry and your toddler falls behind; you yell at him to keep up, he cries, you hit him and say, "I'll give you something to cry about." The value being conveyed is: It is OK to hit/ hurt others when you're frustrated and in a rush. It takes less time and creates a less stressful situation if you take a moment to validate their feelings and explain why you are rushing. "It is difficult for you to keep up because I have longer legs and can walk faster."

Parents are one of the most influential role models in a child's life.

Let's pretend I came into your community for two weeks to secretly videotape you and other parents dropping your children off at school or daycare or while you were in church or shopping. I would do this for the sole purpose of having you realize the types of messages you are teaching your children by your actions, words, tone of voice and facial expressions. Videotaping is a wonderful tool to learn about and improve our behavior.

Viewing a situation after the fact enables us to see ourselves more objectively because the emotional stress has abated.

• Would we see you yelling . . . teaching this is how you gain control.

• Would we see you giving into temper tantrums . . . teaching children to use manipulation rather than words.

• Would we see you expecting perfection . . . teaching it is not OK to make mistakes. OR

• Would we see you being patient, giving explanations . . . teaching them respect.

If you were on this tape would you mind me showing it at a

group presentation? Or would you say, "Please, don't show that to anyone!" (Hmm! Good blackmail technique. Maybe I can afford my nose job after all! ☺) Many people would be embarrassed if I showed the tape, not so much because of what they did, but because others would be watching what they did. Yet, your impressionable, vulnerable children are watching and absorbing your actions. Everyday you are teaching your children values.

Many of us remember hearing from our parents, "Do as I say, not as I do." The fact is children copy what they see on a daily basis. Actions speak louder than words, so as the saying goes, "We need to walk the talk."

If a dentist had yellow rotting teeth and he was teaching the importance of oral hygiene, would you take stock in what he was saying? NO! If you went to a doctor who was smoking up a storm while telling you about the evils of addiction, would you take stock in what he was saying? NO! Yet, how often do parents say one thing and do another.

Take honesty for an example. Nearly everyone wants their children to be honest. Yet a large percentage of adults teach children to lie. (Of course those of us reading this book are not in that large percentage. ☺)

• The phone rings: "Tell them I am not home." Instead of, "Take a message and I will call them back."

• Going to a movie: "Tell them you are only 11 years old so we don't have to pay the full price."

• A birthday party: "Tell everyone you like the gifts they gave even if you don't." Instead of: "Be sure to say thank you for all the gifts you receive."

Many parents value responsibility. They want their children to be responsible for their actions. When children are not, parents get frustrated and wonder why. Well perhaps we should first look at how we modeled this value. They hear us say things like,

"I'm just like my mom, I inherited her thighs and there is nothing I can do about it."

"Yeah, I failed math, my dad failed math and my grandfather failed math. We just don't have good math genes in this family."

"I am so forgetful this morning because I didn't have my coffee."

"I'm in an angry mood because the traffic was so heavy it made me late."

The value being learned is, do not be responsible for your actions or feelings.

It should be no surprise then when children repeat this behavior.

"I failed because the teacher didn't like me."

"I'm grumpy just like my father."

"I was smoking because everyone else was."

"I just lost my temper. I couldn't help it."

We are teaching children to make excuses and blame other people or things instead of taking responsibility for their choices and behaviors.

Daily, we blame outside forces for when we are down or depressed: It's the weather, my boss is on my case, I didn't meet my sales quota, I had a fight with my husband. Then we look outside ourselves for ways to make us feel better:

"I need a drink to relax."

"I'm so nervous I need a cigarette"

"I am so depressed I need some chocolate."

"I am miserable I need to make more money."

Our children, like sponges, absorb all these behaviors and

learn they not only do not have to take responsibility for their actions and feelings, they can also look outside of themselves to feel better and be happy.

We often think the problem with youth is drugs and alcohol. If there weren't drugs and alcohol there would be something else. The problem is, we are raising outer directed children. We raise them to look outside themselves for happiness rather than inside.

Happiness comes from inside, not from outside. Children seem to be learning that in order to be happy they must have "things" like a new pair of sneakers, a new stereo, a cell phone, or a new car. The trouble with "thing" happiness is when the sneakers become scuffed, the stereo becomes old, the cell phone becomes outdated and the car gets its first dent, the happiness disappears and they look for more "things" to fill the void. Or, they may develop the tendency to depend on other events or people to make them happy.

"I'll be happy as soon as I get out of school."

"As soon as I get a job that pays good money, I'll be happy"

"As soon as I get married, I'll be happy."

"Once I have a baby, things will be wonderful."

"As soon as the divorce comes through, things will be great."

The truth is, when we look for material things to make us happy or depend on others to make us happy, our search will never end. We need to realize that happiness comes from within, from loving and respecting ourselves, from making our own choices.

This is what we need to teach children (and ourselves). We have choices and we need to exercise those choices for our own good and happiness. No one can make you unhappy, you choose to be unhappy.

If you were stuck in traffic driving home, you could choose to be angry and annoyed (After all, traffic doesn't care, it won't move any faster because you are upset) or you could choose to put on a tape, read the paper or think over your day. It's your choice. Will you be angry and fume over this rotten traffic or will you distract yourself with something more productive and be in a better mood.

Many years ago I was driving to work in New York City and started to push the play button on my portable cassette player (because my car radio had been stolen). As I went to hit the play button another driver cut in front of me and nearly drove me off the road. I was so upset I forgot about the cassette player. I went to work and if anyone asked how I was I told them I was horrible because I almost got killed. My whole day was spoiled because of this driver. On the way home I went to play my cassette and all I heard was this raving lunatic screaming, yelling and cursing at a driver. That lunatic was me! I had accidentally hit the record button. It made me realize that I had given power over to a total stranger. He was not to blame, I was. It was my choice to allow a stranger to ruin my day. He probably never gave the incident a second thought.

You control your anger; no one else does. If you squeeze an orange, orange juice will come out. It doesn't matter who squeezes the orange, when you squeeze it, or what tool you use to squeeze it, orange juice will come out. It is the same with anger; it doesn't matter who pushed your buttons, when they pushed them or what they used to push them. You're angry at what happened. Acknowledge the anger, find a way to deal with it (confronting, overlooking, giving the benefit of the doubt) and make a choice to move away from it, and stop placing blame on other people or situations for something you have the ability to control. The saying is "When you point the finger of blame at someone else, you are pointing three fingers at yourself."

There is a wonderful story I read in author Dr. Wayne Dwyer's book, *The Sky Is The Limit*.

It is about the alley cat and the kitten. There was this alley cat walking in the alley and he passed a kitten chasing its tale. He walked up to the kitten and said, "Why are you chasing your tale?" The kitten said, "Well, because I just came back from cat philosophy school and I learned two very important things. That happiness is the most important thing in a cat's life and that it is found in my tail. So as soon as I catch my tail I'll be the happiest kitten around." The alley cat thought for a minute and he said "Well, you know, I didn't have the advantage you had of going to cat philosophy school, but hanging out here in the alley, I've learned the same two important things. You are absolutely right. Happiness is the most important thing in a cat's life. And you're right. It is found in our tails. However, I learned if I live my life as I choose, it/happiness follows me wherever I go."

Happiness comes from inside. It comes from accepting and believing in yourself and your strengths. It comes from setting and reaching your own goals, not goals your parents or others thought you should have. Make the choice to be happy.

Often adults think it is too late in life to go after goals that will make them happy.

"I'd like to get another job but that would require going back to school. I can't go back to school I'm 45 now, by the time I am done I'll be 50!" Well, in five years you will still be 50 without the degree and you'll still be unhappy.

My father was the president of his company, making $80,000 a year. (Back then that was a lot of money) We were eight children, some in college and some in private school, yet he left his job because he was not happy and started his own business. He modeled for me that happiness is more important than money. That was a powerful example.

In her late thirties, my mother decided to go college to be a nurse. She spent many hours taking classes, and studying to achieve all her A's. After being an RN for a few years and making lots of money, she realized it was not what she really wanted and pursued another career as a successful counselor. This is another powerful example of modeling persistence. Happiness is more important than money, and it is never too late to go after what you want. (From time to time mom still wonders what she wants to be when she grows up! ☺)

Many of us spend so much of our time either regretting the past or worrying about the future, we miss the present!

Television is another very influential factor in a child's life.

You have all heard the phrase "you are what you eat"; well you are what you watch and what you think about all day long. Most children rely on a mental diet of television, which is pure junk food. It is addictive and they want more. It is mental malnutrition.

In 1950, only 10% of American homes had a television and by 1960 the percentage had grown to 90%. Today 99% of the homes have a television. In fact, more families own a television than a phone. Fifty-four percent of the children in the U.S. have a television set in their bedrooms. Television has become a child's window to their world. It is how they are learning values and beliefs.

In 1992 Neilson Media Research said the average American over a sixty-year lifespan spends ten years in front of the television, two years watching commercials and twenty years sleeping.

In 2000 Neilson Media Research stated that children spend more time learning about life through media than in any other manner. The average child spends approximately 28 hours a week watching television. This is twice as much time as they spend in school. During those hours in front of the TV, they are being very passive. They are sitting back and letting life happen to them rather than making life happen for them.

The average American child will witness over 200,000 acts of violence on television (including 16,000 murders) before age 18. Family hour has now become violence hour because family time is now spent in front of the TV.

There was a study done at Harvard showing that children could not discriminate between reality and fantasy. Amazingly enough, neither could adults. Maybe you remember "Marcus Welby"? Robert Young played a doctor in a TV show. He would get letters from adults saying "I have a pain in my side. What do you think that might be?" He was an actor playing a doctor and adults would write to him for medical advice. Now if adults can't discriminate, can you imagine the difficulty children have?

Consider the negative effects TV has on people. People who watch TV regularly:

• Are rarely satisfied, always thinking they need more things to be happy.

• Seek immediate gratification and quick solutions. All problems are resolved on TV within 30 to 60 minutes. They also learn that commercial products will solve all of their problems.

• Become passive and uninvolved.

• Find violence exciting. The use of violence by music video stars makes it normal and more acceptable behavior.

• Think that skinny is beautiful. When Tahiti finally got TV a few years ago, the young girls who tend to be round and plump, started becoming anorexic.

- Think that you have to be pretty/handsome to be successful.

- Believe happiness comes from material things.

Did you know that watching TV has been linked to obesity in children? And those studies suggest that higher rates of television viewing are correlated with increased tobacco usage, increased alcohol intake and younger onset of sexual activity?

More than 3,000 research projects and scientific studies between the years of 1960 and 1992 confirmed the connection between a steady diet of violent entertainment and aggressive antisocial behavior. There is a definite connection. Televised violence is indeed responsible for a large percentage of the real violence. The crime rate in Canada is very low even though they have more guns per capita than the U.S. and that is because their news shows don't have the same amount of violence. Even though the crime rate has gone down in the U.S., TV news violence has gone up 600%.

A study of population data for various countries showed homicide rates doubling within the 10 to 15 years after the introduction of television, even though television was introduced at different times in each site examined. The media continues to deny this by saying, "No. We have nothing to do with it. We only give people what they want to see."

Remember when cigarette companies said, "There are no connections between smoking and lung cancer?"

What can we do about TV?

1. Plan ahead.

Parents often let their children watch TV in order to have a break, to clean house, entertain company, sleep late, or occupy rainy days. If this is the case, plan ahead. Get a video that is appropriate and is not violent.

2. Make sure that you have inappropriate channels blocked.

3. No violent TV before bedtime.

Many parents allow children to watch TV before bedtime because they feel it is a way of unwinding since they unwind that way. But people dream about what is foremost on their mind before going to bed. Many children wind up having nightmares because they watch so much violence just before going to sleep. Try to make sure that your child doesn't watch TV before bedtime or be sure to monitor what is being watched before bedtime.

4. Watch TV as a family so that you can interpret for your children.

Explain your values about what you are watching. Learn what their perceptions are on what is being viewed. Fifty-five percent of children questioned usually watch television alone or with a friend, but not with their families.

5. Tape TV shows.

Your children can watch shows in less time and not be subjected to the commercials that try to sell a lifestyle.

6. Make certain TV shows off limits.

Allow your child to watch shows that are age appropriate.

They will inevitably say, "My friends are watching it. How come I can't see it?" I once counseled Tony who was seven years old. Before Tony would come into my office, he had to look around to see if "Freddy Krueger" was in there. "Let me check the closet. Let me check under the chairs to see if he is in there." He would not come in until he was sure Freddy was not hiding in the office. He had watched "Friday The 13th" and it nearly scared him to death.

Here is a seven-year-old having nightmares about a movie he should not have been watching. When I asked the mother why she let him watch, her response was,"Well, he wanted to because all of his friends did." Well, most children would eat cookies and milk for dinner every day if you let them, but parents know that is not healthy and would not allow it...why allow them to watch violent shows that are not healthy for them. They are too young to discriminate reality from fantasy. Even adults checked behind the shower curtain after seeing *"Psycho"* by Alfred Hitchcock.

Children try to be cool and tough because their friends watch violent shows and they need to fit in, but you have to be the adult and say no. They'll be thankful for it in the long run. They will use you as an excuse, "Oh, my parents wouldn't let me. I wanted to but they wouldn't let me." When in reality, they may not have wanted to watch in the first place.

7. Use TV punch cards.

Punch Cards are used to help reduce or limit the amount of TV your child watches.

There are two types: one with small TV's in each square and one with numbers in each square. You can color in the TV sets or you can use a hole punch. Explain to your child they are allowed to watch X number of shows per week or watch TV for X number of hours. Each time a show is watched, color in a TV set. Every time an hour is used, hole punch a number. After all the TV sets are colored in or number holes punched, there is no more TV for the week. (Wouldn't some of you like to put your spouses on this system? ☺) The objective is to gradually decrease the amount of time your child spends watching TV. After all the initial whining and complaining, children realize they do not to want to waste their punches on reruns. They are going to look at the program guide and pick out which shows they want to see, or check if any holiday specials are showing. This technique really helps the parent monitor what type of shows their children are selecting.

I would like to share the feedback I received from a parent who used the punch card method. She said: *"I have two children, ages nine and four. My son, age nine, was watching entirely too much TV. He would sit and watch cartoons that he had seen a number of times. It was such a habit for him; I thought I would have a difficult time breaking it, but what a surprise! The first week, each of them had their coupons for twelve shows. They picked their shows carefully. If the show they picked turned out to be a rerun, they didn't waste a punch on it. I was amazed. At the end of the week my son had only watched four shows and my daughter watched six for the entire week. I was amazed at the way it changed their leisure time. Now, five weeks later they are watching about 3-4 shows a week."*

8. Have TV-free nights or days.

These are days where the TV will not be turned on at all. Perhaps no TV during the week and only a few hours on the weekend. Maybe during the week there is only an hour of TV because it is a school night.

How many of us turn away a live person to watch a show? Maybe you'll be watching "ER" on Thursday night and your spouse walks into the room to tell you something about their day and you say, "Shhhh! I've got to see what happens." You turn away a live person to watch this fiction. We find ourselves having conversations about characters on TV shows as if they are real. "Can you believe he cheated on his wife? I hope she finds out." Isn't there enough of that in real life?

We need to monitor how much TV is watched. Children need someone to turn the television off and since we are the role models we need to be the ones to turn it off.

I grew up in a family with eight children. I have six brothers and a sister and we had one TV set so you can imagine the fights that we had. My mother got tired of these fights so she disconnected the TV and told us it was broken and she couldn't afford to fix it. No TV to watch?   What would we do? We quickly learned to say we were going to play outside at the neighbors, but we would really go over and watch TV. My mother caught on and said if you want to play you'll have to be playing outside around the house. We were devastated! What could we possibly do without a TV? Well it didn't take long before we actually started playing together, playing cards, having softball games outside in the neighborhood. It changed the way we spent our free time together. Now, as adults, out of eight children, seven of us have our own businesses. I believe not having a TV played an important part in that because we had to make things happen for ourselves. We had to take the initiative to entertain ourselves and be productive rather than sitting in front of the TV being passive and uninvolved. Parents need to be the one to turn the TV off.

Current facts about media violence and effects on the American Family.

Polls show that three-quarters of the public find television entertainment too violent. When asked to select measures which would reduce violent crime, a lot of Americans chose restrictions on television violence more often than gun control.

Studies tracking viewing habits and behavior patterns of a single individual found that 8-year-old boys who viewed the most violent programs growing up were the most likely to engage in aggressive and delinquent behavior by age 18 and serious criminal behavior by age 30.

Potential adverse effects of excessive exposure to media include: increased violent behavior, obesity, decreased physical activity and fitness, increased cholesterol levels and sodium intake; repetitive strain injury (video computer games); insomnia; impaired school performance; increased sexual activity and use of tobacco and alcohol; decreased attention span; decreased family communication; desensitization; and excess consumer focus.

According to the National Television Violence Study, the context in which violence is portrayed is as important to its impact as the amount of violence. The study concluded that 66% of children's programming had violence. Of the shows with violent content, three-quarters demonstrated unpunished violence and when violence occurred; 58% of the time victims were not shown experiencing pain.

Forty-six percent of all television violence identified by the study took place in children's cartoons. Children's programs were least likely to depict the long-term consequences of violence (5%) and they portray violence in a humorous fashion 67% of the time.

The use of parental warnings and violence advisories made the programs more of a magnet than they might otherwise have been. Parental Discretion Advised and PG-13 and R ratings significantly increased.

MTV celebrated its 20th birthday in 2001. Many in the entertainment industry refer to those younger than 20 as "MTV babies," because MTV had a major impact on the way TV programs are produced.

MTV pioneered the fast paced, "in your face" style of programming and advertising. With quick cuts, layered graphics, multiple messages, loud audio, high impact visuals, frenetic bursts, and random transitions, this style has affected programming of every media type.

Did you know?

MTV globally reaches 350 million households (PBS On-Line, 2001).

MTV has been a very successful business because it is almost non-stop advertising. In addition to the traditional commercials, the videos themselves promote new albums.

82% of MTV viewers are 12 to 34 years old, with 39% under the age of eighteen (Nielson Media Research, 2000).

Music videos are designed for teenagers between 12 and 19 years of age (Rich, 1998).

73% of boys and 78% of girls in the 12 to 19 years of age group watch MTV. Boys watch for an average of 6.6 hours per week and girls watch for an average of 6.2 hours per week (Rich, 1998).

MTV is the most recognized network among young adults ages 12 to 34 (Nielson Media Research, 2000).

Sexual Imagery, Violence, Alcohol and Tobacco Portrayal in Music Videos:

In one study 75% of concept music videos (those that told a story) involve sexual imagery and more than half involve violence - usually against women (Pediatrics, 2001).

An analysis of music videos found that nearly one-fourth of all MTV videos portray overt violence and depict weapon carrying with attractive role models being aggressors in more than 80% of the violent videos (DuRant, 1997).

One-fourth of all MTV videos contain alcohol or tobacco use (DuRant, 1997).

A longitudinal study found a positive correlation between TV and music video viewing and alcohol consumption among teens (Robinson, 1998).

The Effects

According to some research, even modest viewing of MTV and other music videos results in significant exposure to glamorized depictions of alcohol and tobacco use, violence and weapons.

When lyrics are acted out in a story-telling music video, their impact is enhanced.

Music videos appear to contribute to teens' desensitization to violence.

At least two experiments show that watching MTV results in more permissive attitudes about sex. One of these (Calfin, Carroll, & Schmidt, 1993) found that college students who were assigned to watch MTV developed more liberal attitudes toward premarital sex than their peers who did not watch MTV as part of the study.

I hope this is enough to convince you to reduce your child's time in front of the TV . . . otherwise known as the boob tube!

The above information was taken from the Neilson Medial web site.

"I'm Your Kid, Just Show Me."

I'd rather see a lesson than just hear one anyday,
I'd rather you should walk with me than merely point the way;
For the eye's a better learner and more willing than the ear,
Your words can be confusing; but your example's always clear:!
For the best of parents, teachers, kings . . . are those who live their creed,
And to see good put into action, is what I really need.
I can learn what all I should be; just show me how it's done;
I can follow every move you make; your words too fast may run.
And those lectures you deliver may be very wise and true,
But I'm more apt to learn my lesson by observing what you do.
For I may misunderstand you in the great advice you give,
But there's no misunderstanding when I see the way you live!

6

☺ ☺ ☺

"CONSTRUCTIVE CRITISM . . . . IS THERE SUCH A THING?

*When it comes to criticism many of us believe
it is better to give than to receive.*

Why do we criticize our children?

By criticizing, we think we are doing them a favor, helping
them identify their inappropriate behavior so that they can
mend the error of their ways
and become more successful
and more perfect like us! ☺
Who else is going to tell them
they have bad breath, have no
manners, shouldn't be a dancer,
look fat, or got a bad haircut.
After all, isn't it the parent's
job to be honest and make the
child aware of their weaknesses
and shortcomings so they don't
embarrass themselves, or so
they can change?

AND HON, I'M NOT A
PSYCHIATRIST OR ANYTHING,
BUT I'M GUESSING THAT
THINGS MIGHT BE A LITTLE
LESS STORMY WITH OUR
TEENAGE SON IF YOU
STOPPED REFERRING TO
HIM AS "YOU DECEITFUL
LITTLE SNOT-NOSED
WEASEL."

**Sharing your feelings with your children is
important to good parenting.**

I have heard criticism referred to as "killer talk" because it
tends to kill communication and openness between people.
It is used to tell other people, indirectly, that you are hurt,
frightened, or disappointed. However, the receiver won't be
able to hear your message because you aren't sharing your
hurt feelings, but rather attacking them. The receiver's ears
tend to close in order to protect themselves from the hurt.
Also, the receiver can't listen to your message because they
are preparing their counter attack.

Yet we need criticism because:

- It gives us feedback on what is working and what is not.

- Without criticism, minor problems go unsolved and often grow into major crises

- When used correctly, we can grow and learn from it

Q. If criticism is so helpful then why do people cringe when they hear it?

A. We think criticism and disapproval are synonyms but they are not.

Q. Why do we resist taking full advantage of what can be such an enormous benefit?

A. Self-image is based on how others view us. When we find that someone sees us in a less than positive light, we can feel devastated.

Shad Helmstead, the author of *The Self-Talk Solution*, explains self-esteem as a huge room filled with filing cabinets from floor to ceiling. In every one of those files is every thought, every experience a person has ever had from the time that they were small. Picture a baby's filing room. They have millions of filing cabinets. If you opened every drawer you would find them all to be empty, except for one.

In that one filing cabinet there would be files for safety, food and warmth. If you were to go back into that room/child's mind, when that child was six, twelve, sixteen, or when that child was an adult, you would find every filing cabinet jammed packed with files.

Most of the files were put there by other people. Those cabinets contain other people's comments to you, reactions to you, and judgments of you.

It doesn't matter whether the information

put in the files is true or false or good or bad. The child/adult will live their life according to the information that is in their filing cabinets.

The files in a person's cabinet will guide the person's future. Unfortunately, most of them are the wrong files and shouldn't be there. Those files form the basis of what a child will expect from life, how he will deal with problems, how he will get along with others.

If a child has negative files he will have a negative image of himself. He will attract negative situations in life.

We need to teach our children and ourselves how to go through those filing cabinets, clean them out and get rid of the programmed negative images. There are some files that don't help you. Throw them away. Burn them. Replace them with positive files so that you can have a more positive experience and attract more positive images about yourself.

In the next chapter we will look at how children and adults can change those files, but first let's look at how those files get stored in one's filing cabinet in the first place.

Program files are placed in a child's filing cabinet by parents, siblings, classmates, teachers, relatives, music and television. A child's subconscious mind listens to each message it receives, looks for other similar files or beliefs that this new piece of information supports and then stores it. The files that are repeated the most often are the ones which take over a child's mind.

Imagine what the future results of the following negative comments would be:

You're impossible.

Your room is always a mess.

Why should I believe you?

You just don't try.

What makes you think you're so special?

All you know how to do is cause problems.

All you ever do is argue.

Talking to you is like talking to a brick wall.

You never tell me the truth.

I've had it with you.

You never care about anyone but yourself.

You just don't think.

Your brother never talks to me like that.

What did I ever do to deserve this?

Who do you think you are?

Now why would caring loving parents say such things?

1. We are human and get frustrated.

2. We don't realize or think about the impact.

3. We think, as the parent, we are the people that need to tell the child honestly what they are doing wrong.

An example can be found in a story Zig Ziglar tells about a sixteen- year old boy named Victor Cerebreokoff. An adult, a voice of authority, told him "Victor, you're a dunce. You're a failure in school. You're not doing well. You're not going to be very successful. You would be better off dropping out of school and learning a trade." Victor listened to this voice of authority. He dropped out of school. He put a file in his "filing" cabinet stating he was a dunce and would not be successful. Therefore every morning he got up and he looked in the mirror and he saw a dunce, he shaved a dunce, he dressed a dunce. He took odd jobs. He jumped from one job to another, knowing that he was not really talented or smart enough to hold down a good job. Finally he decided to join the army. He had to take an IQ test. The sergeant called him in and he said to him, "You know what, Victor? You're a genius. You have an IQ of 161." Nothing else changed in Victor's life other than the information that went into his mind, which created a new file. From that point on when Victor got up in the morning, he looked in the mirror and he saw a genius. He dressed a genius. He shaved a genius. Victor went on to become a successful businessman, author...and the president of the Mensa Society. (Where you have to have an IQ of 150 just to get in)

All too often, adults put negative information/files into a child's mind. The child believes the information, stores it, acts upon it and then adults wonder why children do the things they do!

Many parents say that they love their children. But do their children know it? Do they feel it through their words and actions? Parents often say one thing but their words, actions, and tone of voice convey another. They tell their children they love them yet they continuously criticize them. These are mixed messages that are very confusing to a child.

Criticism is by far the most damaging thing we do to each other and our children. It is the negative file we most often put in our children's file cabinet, without realizing it. Knowing this, we need to take a detailed look at the effects of criticism. You may not realize that as parents you are the most important and most influential person in your child's life. This is why children are so sensitive to what you say to them. They evaluate themselves based on the opinions you have of them. They take your criticism personally.

Let's look at what the original purpose of criticism was:

Originally, criticism was meant to be an appraisal of ideas and actions. The critic was expected to assess the merits as well as demerits. The goal of the critic was to communicate, influence and motivate. The dictionary defines criticism as a way to communicate information to another in a way that enables one to use it to their advantage and benefit. It is a tool to encourage and enhance personal growth. The message behind criticism is supposed to be, "I am telling you this because I think it can help you and our relationship."

So tell me, when your boss calls you in and says, "I have some constructive criticism for you, are you thinking "Yeah! This is great! I'm being given a chance to get some good tools for personal growth"! I would guess it is more likely that you would be dreading hearing what he has to say.

If you cooked dinner and a family member said to you, "This is a terrible dinner you've cooked." What would your response be?

1) I am glad you told me; I will try to cook a better dinner tomorrow.

2) Cook it yourself.

3) Take me out to dinner.

4) Throw the dinner at them.

They were just giving you constructive criticism so that you wouldn't cook such a lousy dinner the next time. You mean to tell me that criticism didn't motivate you to improve your cooking skills? ☺

Perhaps they didn't say it in a loving tone of voice.

Let's try another example:

Your spouse approaches you and says in a loving, caring tone, "Honey, I know we have a very good relationship. I love you very much. I want to tell you something because I believe it will just improve our relationship. I don't want you to be hurt or upset and don't take it personally; it is just that I want us to be as good as we can be. I just want you to know that you are a boring bed partner and need to be more active."

Did this criticism, said in loving way, motivate you to improve? Are you ready, after that, to jump back into the sack and try to improve yourself? Or would you withdraw or get angry?

Your child reacts in the same way when you say, "This room is a pigsty. You're such a slob!" Is that supposed to motivate them to improve?

People will often tell me I shouldn't compare the extreme example of the bedroom to keeping a room clean, because the bedroom issue is a more sensitive issue. But I must tell you to a child the hurt is just the same.

"I don't like your friends, I don't like your hairstyle, you have horrible handwriting" hurts a child just as much as "You're a boring bed partner" hurts an adult. And it produces the same result-- avoidance, anger, resentment, and embarrassment. Criticism is especially damaging when it comes from someone we love and trust. It is like taking a sledgehammer to a piece of crystal. It makes shards of our confidence and motivation. In my opinion, criticism, as it is used today, is not constructive.

A study done at the University of Calgary showed that constant verbal abuse was likely to do more damage than physical abuse because we are constantly planting seeds of doubt in our child's mind. The underlying message of any criticism is: you are incompetent, unlovable; who you are is not enough. Constant criticism makes a child feel powerless, unimportant and inadequate. They soon believe they are bad and can never do enough to earn your love; their self-esteem crumbles.

Maybe you had a perfectionist parent and you were constantly trying to please them. However, they were constantly picking on the little things and no matter what you did it was not enough. So you did one of two things:

1. Gave up and stopped trying, thinking, "Why bother, it is never right anyway."

2. You became a perfectionist or an overachiever in attempts to get that approval.

Again we don't criticize others to hurt them, we think we are helping. Read the comments below. If they were said to you, would it add pieces to your IALAC sign or rip it to pieces?

When are you going to grow up and act your age?

You are such a slow poke.

How are you ever going to amount to anything?

What do you mean you can't do that? Anyone could do that.

What are you . . . brain dead?

Why don't you stick to something you're good at? Singing isn't one of them!

I would have done it an easier way.

You really don't need that piece of cake, do you?

Why don't you let someone with more experience do it?

I expect more from you. You are older.

Those pants make you look heavier than you are.

Can't you do anything right?

You'll be the death of me yet.

You're going out looking like that?

If you would slow down, you might do a half-way decent job.

Is that your best?

I know you could do better.

Let's just look at the last two statements.

IS THAT YOUR BEST?
Obviously you don't think so.

I KNOW YOU COULD DO BETTER?
Obviously, what I have done is not good enough.

The problem with all of the above statements is that they attack the person, not the problem, and they don't tell the person what to do to be successful in the future. We're criticizing the child for something in the past, something that has already been done. We can't change the past but we can change tomorrow. Don't remind the child how bad she was while food shopping last week. Tell her what you expect from her this week.

Before I talk about how to give constructive criticism let's look at the effects of destructive criticism.

LONG TERM EFFECTS OF DESTRUCTIVE CRITICISM

1. Destructive criticism makes a child avoid the critical person or situation.

If a father constantly criticizes his son, the child will most likely go to great lengths to avoid contact with the father and only seek help from the mother.

Children who are criticized often in one area will usually avoid those situations. For example:

A girl at her softball game needed to catch the ball that would end the game, but she missed it. While driving home her mom or dad said, "You know anybody could have caught that ball. I can't believe you missed it. You don't pay attention." Do you think that child will want her mom or dad to show up at her next ballgame? Will she even want to play softball next year? Probably not, because the child doesn't want to be a disappointment to her parents, nor does she want to be put in situations where she is ridiculed and made to feel inadequate.

Many adults avoid certain relatives at family events and

even avoid events because they are continually asked, "Are you ever going to get married? Are you even dating anyone?"

This can be interpreted to mean, "You are a nobody and a loser because you can't find yourself a mate."   My mom had an aunt that she avoided like the plague because every time she saw her, after the welcoming hello, how are you, it's so good to see you, followed, "You haven't lost any weight, have you?

2.   A child will imitate the critical behavior.

A child who receives a great deal of destructive criticism tends to develop the habit of critiquing others. A child will imitate the critical behavior. They are constantly around criticism and it becomes a part of them. In the same way a child learns to talk by hearing adults speak over and over, they learn to repeat what adults say and how they say it.

I have a friend who is very negative about her husband and children. She constantly criticizes their efforts and actions and rarely says anything positive. I went to her house for a party and her mother was there. It was at that point I understood why my friend was the way she was. Every little thing my friend did was criticized, put down, and made fun of. The house was not clean enough, the food was overcooked, the kids were not dressed appropriately, the curtains didn't match the couch. I could understand where her behavior came from. When her mom left the party she said, "Oh, my mother is so negative. She is always criticizing every thing I do." Isn't that interesting? She can see it in her mother but not in herself. She exhibits the same, exact behavior to her children and that same behavior is going to be passed on to their children. It is important for us to begin to break these cycles.

3. Destructive criticism makes a child less likely to try new behaviors.

A child will be less likely to try new behaviors because he fears criticism by those who are important to him.

Here are some examples:

You baked a cake and your child was helping you decorate it and made some kind of shape that was supposed to be a letter; you said, "Oh, you ruined it now." Even though the child was attempting to help and be creative, the chances are they will not want to help again for fear of ruining the cake.

Maybe your teenage daughter decided that she was going to cook dinner for the family. After tasting it you said, "My gosh, I had better food in the army." They may not be too willing to try their hand at cooking again because of that criticism.

Your child decided to dress herself for school and came downstairs to show you, "Look mom I did it all by myself." You responded by saying, "Oh no, that doesn't match. You can't go to school like that. Let's go and change. I'll pick out something better." Now you'll be dressing your child for the rest of your life! ☺

4. Destructive criticism damages the self-esteem of the child and the parent.

The child's self-esteem is damaged because they are having repeated failures pointed out. The parent's self-esteem is damaged because they take the blame for the child's behavior. "I must not be a very good parent otherwise my child wouldn't misbehave."

GUIDELINES TO USING EFFECTIVE CRITICISM

1. Be sure the behavior can be changed

We often get annoyed with children because they don't handle things the way we want them to. It may be because they don't have the skill level to do so. Most children will pick up appropriate social skills from watching adults, siblings and classmates.

Some children lack the specific skills and need to be taught in a more formal but fun way.

For example:

You might have a tea party to teach table manners, or play school to teach a child how to follow directions or make friends.

2. Focus on the deed, not the doer. Get rid of the behavior, not the person.

Don't attack personality attributes or criticize character traits.

For example: "You careless idiot, you spilled the last of the milk."

Instead describe the situation at hand.

This is the key to constructive criticism or, as I would prefer to call it, "constructive feedback".

Describe What Needs To Be Done In The Future In Order To Be Successful.

Again, we can't change the past, we can't erase the mistake we've already made, but we can learn from it and behave correctly in the future.

For example:

• Instead of saying, "You are such slob, you never clean up after yourself."

You can say, "When you are done making your snack, you need to put the dishes in the dishwasher."

• Instead of saying, "You haven't taken the dog out all day--you don't deserve a pet."

You can say, "The dog is pacing by the door. You need to take him outside."

• And instead of saying, "Are you brain dead? How many times do I have to tell you to turn out the lights?

What am I the electric company?"

Try saying something like "When you leave the bathroom, turn out the lights."

Describing is the first part, leaving off the insult at the end is the second and most difficult part.

"Dirty clothes belong in the clothes basket – YOU'LL NEVER LEARN!

Perhaps leaving a note would be helpful in keeping the anger out of your words.

I realize this is an easy skill to speak about but a very difficult skill to put into practice when you are annoyed. It takes time, but like anything else if you practice it often, no matter how unlike you it may sound, it becomes part of you. Keep in mind the end result you want? **Do you want to get your frustration out and make your child feel stupid or do you want the behavior to change?**

In the above examples, the first statement will close a child off from listening to you. The second will let them know what is expected.

You may be thinking, "Well I have tried this and have repeated myself 100 times. They still leave the lights on."

• Repetition is how children learn so it may take 120 times before they remember. (How many times did you say the word 'mommy' before your child repeated correctly?)

• After time you will need to fall back on your discipline plan (that will be in the next book!)

What have you got to lose by trying it? Has anything else worked so far?

Describe, instead of criticize, the following statements. (HINT: State the behavior you want in the future)

You are so selfish!

You are eating like a pig!

Shut your mouth when I'm talking!

(Answers: You need to take turns with the crayons; Please chew with your mouth closed; Be quiet and wait until I am finished speaking.)

3. Monitor your tone of voice and body language

Hands on hips, fingers pointing in a child's face, arms crossed over your chest, yelling, and sarcastic tone of voice, all put a child on the defensive and they shut down. Once you get the right words down then work on your body language. I believe in working on one thing at a time otherwise you get overwhelmed and give up.

4. Timing and place is critical

Check out the emotional climate before opening your mouth.

Did your child just try really hard to do something to please you but instead of recognizing the effort you point out what they did not do? Example:

Your child just cleaned his room and wants you to come in and look at how well he cleaned it.

You see the clothes have been picked up but the floor has not been vacuumed. Don't say anything about the vacuuming at this time. Simply state, "I see you have gotten all the clothes off the floor." Period. The next time you ask your child to clean his room say, "I would like you to clean your room, first by picking the clothes off the floor then by vacuuming.

You may ask, "Well what if I can't wait unil the next time. I need it done right way because I have company coming over" In this case you say, " I see you have started to clean your room by getting all the clothes off the floor, the next step is to vacuum." Describe what you want the next time the stiuation comes up rather than bursting their bubble and causing resentment.

When I was first married and my husband washed the dishes, it was very nice but he never emptied out the drain where all the gook is. He never did it and it would drive me crazy. I wanted to just scream, "If you're going to do the dishes, why can't you just empty out the strainer when you do it?" But, if I criticized, what would he have done? He wouldn't do the dishes anymore! (A fate worse than death for me! ☺) What I could have done was wait until the next time he did the dishes and say, "Thanks for doing the dishes. Could you also empty out the strainer when you're done?" The difficult part is leaving off, "because you didn't do it last time!"

5. Use words that the child understands

Sometimes we forget that a child does not understand the words we are using, so they misunderstand why they are getting criticized.

A perfect example:

I once had a class of 5-year-old children. I taught them about goal setting, because nothing builds self-esteem like success. You have success if you set a goal and reach it. Every student and teacher has to choose a goal, a behavior that they want to improve on, so we can be a better person and be happier. Jeremy reached his first goal and it was time for him choose a new goal. I asked, "Jeremy, what is your new goal going to be?" He said "Well, I got to change my attitude." He is 5 years old! How does he know what attitude is? I questioned, "Jeremy, exactly what do you mean by 'attitude'?" He said, "I don't know. My mom's always saying 'you got a bad attitude. You better change it!'" ☺ Jeremy knew there was something his mom didn't like about him, or that she didn't approve of, but didn't know what it was or how to fix it and yet knew he was not loved/accepted for it.

Be sure to describe what you want in words children

understand. It also helps to provide young children with examples.

6. Have age appropriate expectations

Don't expect your 4 year old to clean the room like you would clean it. For that matter, don't expect your 16 year old to clean the room like you would want it cleaned. ☺ This is where you have to let them know specifically what you want. Don't say, "Go clean your room" because to them their room is clean. Everything that was out is now under the bed and stuffed into the closets. That is clean to a child; what more could you possibly want?

Rather than becoming frustrated, angry and start criticizing them, how about saying, "I need everything off the floors, folded and put in your drawers." Younger children will need it broken down into even simpler terms. You have to be very specific with what you want them to do and break it down. You may say, "We have three jobs to do in your room. I'll give you the first one, when that is done come back and I will give you the second one." etc.

SUCCESS BUILDS SELF-ESTEEM

Too often we set children up for failure:

One day my niece came over for a visit. We had a big bin of Legos® She wanted to dump the entire bin of Legos on the floor. I agreed as long as she agreed to put them all back in the bin.

Naturally when it came time to put them away she did not want to help. I attempted to use my child psychology. I tried the "beat the clock technique." "Let's see if you can get all the Legos in the bin before the timer goes off." At first she was excited. She took her little 5-year-old hand, picked up a few Legos pieces, ran over to the bin and dropped them in. She did this two more times, then stopped and looked at me and said, "You know what, Aunt MaryAnn? I don't care if I beat the time clock." So much for those psychology books! ☺

Then I realized that it was a big task for a 5 year old to do. Plus the way she was doing it would take forever for her to complete. I had set her up for failure. What I had to do was show her how she could complete the task. How to move the bin right next to the Legos, use the top of the bin to scoop up the Legos and then pour them right into the bin. That way she could beat the timer.

Be proactive when you ask a child to do a task, make sure that you are setting them up for success by explaining and demonstrating exactly how it can be done.

7. Be honest

Stay away from words such as "always" and "never". Words like "always" and "never" are very hurtful. "You are always late for dinner." "You never come home on time." Now, I doubt that a person can always be late–every single time. There had to be at least one time that they were on time so when you say the words "you're always late" it negates the one time that they were on time. It says, well, she didn't even notice the few times I was on time so why even consider being on time anymore. Or, it starts an argument, "Yes I was. Don't you remember last June 22nd? I came home from the concert on time; I was even 15 minutes early!"

We do this with our spouses. We say things such as, "You never bring flowers home for me." Your spouse says, "Yes I do; remember back in 1979...". the response is arguing the 'never' part. What you are really trying to say is, "I would like you to bring me flowers more often." Say what you want and stay away from the generalizations "never" and "always".

8. Think before you talk

I heard of one mother saying, "If you hit your brother again, I will cut that hand off and hit you with it." Many times bizarre comments spew out of parents mouths when they are frustrated and don't have a plan.

When you are in the car and your children are arguing about who is touching their side of the seat, what do many parents do? Stop the car and say, "If I have to pull this car over you'll be sorry." Or, "That's it! One more sound and I'm going to make you get out and walk home." How many people have said something like that? How many people have actually stopped and made them walk home? That is what happens when we don't think before we speak. We end up threatening. A threat is usually something we are not willing or able to follow through on. In my discipline workshops for parents we talk about how having a plan ahead of time can save you a lot of aggravation later. We all know when you put two or more children in the back seat for a period of time an argument is sure to break out.

To prevent situations like this from happening you need to plan ahead.

• Be proactive to avoid the problem from occurring in the first place

• What will you do if a problem does occur?

• What consequences are you willing to set up and follow through on?

• Inform the child of the plan before the situation arises.

One mother told me she had a plan; she kept a fly swatter on the front seat, and, if they acted out, she swatted them. ☺ It is a plan, but not one I recommend. I would recommend having car games that stay just in the car. Explain to your children what your expectations are and what the consequences are before you get in the car, such as: "If you argue for 10 minutes you will go to bed 10 minutes earlier tonight."

9. Use outside sources

There are times when no matter how well you give constructive feedback your children won't listen to it because it comes from you–their parents. They feel, "Oh, that's just my mother or my father telling me that. It's not really true." If you get their favorite aunt, teacher, or friend to tell them the same exact thing, they'll believe it. If you have a teenager and you try to teach them not to smoke or drink, they probably won't listen to you. But perhaps one of their favorite movie stars or musical groups has an article on the dangers of smoking or drinking that you can have them read. Your child will probably be more likely to at least entertain their ideas. My point: Your message is not being heard, so find another way. Let go of your pride and accept that sometimes children (and even adults) are just more receptive when they hear the message from another person, maybe someone who is not as personally involved as you are. Don't be upset they didn't listen to you; be grateful they heard the message. Children don't welcome parental criticism because it means admitting they are wrong and they need to save face. This way the child feels like they are agreeing with an expert rather than giving in to authority.

10. Use analogies from their own life or books they've read

Use a child's past experience to help them understand the present:

Let's say your child is having trouble in math and plays tennis as an extracurricular activity.

You say, "I remember when you first started your tennis lessons. You were having trouble with your backhand so you went to your coach. He practiced your backhand with you for 15 minutes everyday and now you have a great backhand. I'm wondering if that would work with your math. We could work together on your math for a half hour a day."

Young children often think that when a parent punishes them it means they don't love them. Refer back when you first owned a dog and he was a puppy. "Remember when the puppy ran out into the middle of the road and we rolled up the newspaper and lightly hit him on his hind end. Did we do that because we didn't love him?" The child responds, "No. We didn't want him to run into the middle of the road and get hit by a car." "Well, that is why mommy has you in the time-out chair, because you chose to touch the stove or not to listen and that was not safe for you." Choose analogies that a child can relate to.

Use storybooks for analogies. There is a story called "Everybody Hates Harold". This story talks about a boy in school who is not well liked, why, and what he does to change. If your child is having trouble in school it may be difficult to discuss it in the first person. It would be difficult to ask, "Why doesn't anyone like you?" without the child being hurt or defensive. However, you could read the book to your child and when similar situations come up, say, "I remember when that happened to Harold. He felt... Is that how you feel? Do you think it might help to try...like Harold did?"

11. Reverse roles

You and your child may see things from different perspectives. Try reversing roles with them. Have your child be you and you be the child. If done correctly, this can be a real eye opener for the child.

A friend of mine did this with her girls at dinnertime. The girls were always complaining about dinner and whining throughout the entire meal. So they switched roles. The parents became the girls and the girls became the parents:

Parents, "Ewe! We're having peas again? I can't stand peas!

112

We always have peas. Whoever invented these things anyhow? Why do we have to eat something we hate? You don't love us because you make us eat these things. Yuk!"

After a short time the girls became frustrated and said, "Stop! We don't want to play anymore." It was good for them to see what it was like for their parents. From there it would be ideal to have a discussion or brainstorming session and find a workable solution for all.

Another idea is to, with their knowledge, video tape or audio tape your child. It is more objective and they can see exactly what behavior you are referring to. If you have a child who has temper tantrums, picks on younger siblings, or uses a baby voice, let them listen to how they sound or see what they do. The tape is not to prove you are right or to punish the child; it is meant to be used as a learning tool to let them see things from another perspective and come up with alternative ideas.

It is a great tool for parents to use for themselves as well—if you are brave enough to watch yourself. ☺

12. Do not combine praise with criticism

If a child brought home a report card with mostly A's and one C, what do we do? We criticize the one C rather than focusing on all those A's and the good work they did. Why not let that child bask in the victory of the A's that they have? "I'm proud of your accomplishment. You have four A's! Let's make your favorite dinner." Or, "Let's make popcorn and watch a movie."

Yikes! What about the C? Do you have to say something? That C isn't going anywhere. What's your rush? In a week, or even two weeks you can approach the subject and say, "According to your grade in math you are having some trouble. Is there anything we can do to help you improve that?" (Notice, I didn't say you're failing, you don't try hard enough, you stink in math, you are as bad as your father in math, and we don't have math genes in our family.) If they don't have suggestions say, "Here are some things I've heard other children try when they need help in math.....which one would work for you?"

Imagine your boss called you in to her office to praise you on your handling of an account and then proceeded to tell you how poorly your paper work was done. What is the one thing you remember when you leave?

13. Give one-minute criticisms

• **Be specific by describing** - Don't say, "I'm really angry - you should know why, you're so clumsy, so irresponsible."

Get right to the point of what the concern is: "You didn't come home right after school with the car like you promised."

• **State how you feel about what they did wrong.**

Don't say, "You messed up last week, you can't be trusted. I don't think you deserve the use of the car anymore..."

Say: "I am very upset, because it made me late for my appointment and your brother missed his ball game."

• **Tell them specifically what you want them to do the next time**

"I need you to come home at the time we agreed upon."

• **Reaffirm the person**

"This is not like you. I know you are a responsible child, I know you are capable of doing this. I'm looking forward to the next time you go out and I can count on you to be back with the car on time."

This shows them that you have faith in them, that when (and if ☺) you ever let them have that car again, that they will be able to be back on time. You are not attacking the person, just the behavior and the situation.

114

Another alternative is listening to your child's side of the situation and asking only 3 questions :

1. What do you think happened?

   Ex: It was very foggy out - I couldn't see very well.

   Ex: I drew on the wall. I wanted to make a picture.

2. What could you have done so this wouldn't have happened?

   Ex: I could have driven more slowly or called you to pick me up.

   Ex: I could have asked you for paper.

3. What are you going to do about it?

   Ex: Get a job to help pay for the repairs.

   Ex: Wash the wall.

14. Give permission to make mistakes. Mistakes are a way to learn:

Often parents criticize mistakes in an attempt to motivate children to improve, not realizing that constant criticism provokes rebellion instead of inspiring improvement.

Parents criticize mistakes largely due to fear:

Fear that they aren't doing a good job parenting.

Fear of what the " neighbors" will think.

Fear because they don't know what else do.

Fear that if they don't humiliate and shame their child, they won't learn.

It is believed that when adults feel such fear they cover it up by acting more controlling. It is important to teach our children as well as ourselves that mistakes are opportunities to learn.

When you have a child that is starting to talk they are learning words. They might say something like, "wa-wa," meaning 'water' and parents get all excited. "Oh my gosh! He's talking. Isn't this great?! Did you hear him? Say it again. Let's call up Grandma. Grandma, listen!" The child says it again and you hug and kiss him. You are so thrilled! You continue to encourage him until eventually he learns to say the word correctly.

Now the child is six years old and decides to be brave and try something new. He takes a gallon of milk and pours it in his cereal. Only, this time he wasn't as successful and it spilled all over the floor. Are you still saying, "Let's call Grandma?" Probably, but not for the same reason and not before you criticize them for spilling milk while trying to do something new on their own. You still call her but this time it is to complain. Oh, how wonderful it is when you call your parents to complain about your children. Their response is the inevitable "mother's curse"; "I told you when you grew up and had children, you'd have one just like you"! (So much for support.) ☺

To avoid the child making future mistakes take time to teach them the skills they need to be successful rather than just criticizing the behavior out of frustration.

Marvin Marshall the author of *Discipline Without Stress* has a saying I treasure and it applies here:

"YOU CAN'T BE PERFECT AND LEARN AT THE SAME TIME."

Here is a poem that summarizes what we have been discussing in regard to mistakes and criticism with children.

THE COURAGE TO BE IMPERFECT
by Rudolf Dreikurs

. . . . It seems to me that our children are exposed to a sequence of discouraging experiences, both at home and at school. Everyone points out what they did wrong and what they could do wrong. We deprive children of the only experience which can really promote growth and development–experience of their own strengths. We impress them with their deficiencies, with their smallness, with their limitations, and at the same time try to drive them on to be much more. If we want to institute in children the desire to accomplish something, a faith in themselves and a regard for their own strengths, then we have to minimize the importance of the mistakes they are making and emphasize all the good things-not what they could do, but what they do do....

. . . . We become overly impressed by everything that is wrong in us and around us: "If I am critical of myself, I naturally am going to be critical of the people around me. If I am sure that I am no good, at least I have to find that you are worse." That is what we are doing. Anyone who is critical of himself is always critical of others. To be human does not mean to be right, does not mean to be perfect. To be human means to be useful, to make contributions-not for oneself, but for others–to take what there is and to make the best out of it.

ADULTS RECEIVING CRITICISM

Let's look at what we can do for ourselves because our spouses, parents, bosses and even our own children criticize us all the time. When on the receiving end of criticism; look at three areas:

1. How important is the criticism

Ask yourself. How important is this criticism to me? If somebody criticizes your shoes - well your feet are under a desk all day so it's not important. You won't worry too much about it. If they criticized the way you work with children and that is your livelihood . . . that might be important enough to look into changing, because criticisms that are important determine how much energy you will put into changing your behavior. If it is affecting your job or affecting your children, then you may want to put a lot of energy into changing the behavior. If it is not really important, and you don't feel the need to change, then don't put any energy into it.

2. Appraise the validity of the criticism

Is the critic knowledgeable and experienced in this area?

Let's say I'm an engineer and somebody who doesn't know anything about engineering criticizes my performance. They need to have some knowledge or some background for there to be any validity to what they are saying.

3. Gauge the emotional climate

Did something just happen that made the critic upset or hurt, and they are taking it out on the wrong person? If your boss came in hot and angry and said, "You are a lousy worker", you may ask yourself, "Is it because his boss just came down on him so he is taking it out on me?"

If your boss came in calmly to speak with you and said, "You're a lousy worker", you might put a little more stock in it. But, first you would need more details because 'lousy' doesn't tell you what needs to be changed.

I am always amazed at how we allow people to come into our homes and into our lives and just rip our sign, or dump garbage (destructive criticism) on us, and we don't stand up for ourselves. We let them criticize us and we accept it and store it in our filing cabinet. It is important not to let people dump garbage on you!

We will go to a family party and a relative will say something hurtful. Instead of saying something to that relative, we go home and call everyone else in the family and tell them about what was said.

When someone criticizes you in a destructive way, when they give you a zinger, don't keep those hurt feelings inside trying to guess why they did that. Instead try one of the following ideas:

1. Ask, "Why did you say that? What was your purpose for making that comment?"

What this question does is make the critic clarify the reason. It makes them think more carefully about the words they choose. It helps them to be more descriptive. It also helps to clear up any misperceptions you may have had about the comment.

When your mother-in-law comes in and tells you that you don't know how to keep a house or cook, ask, "Why did you say that?" Of course your mother-in-law might say, "Because you are a slob. You don't know how to keep a house." If this happens you go to the next step, which is to ask:

2. "Did you say that to hurt me?" or "Did you say that to offend/insult me?"

When some people criticize us, they think they are helping and they don't realize they are hurting us. Of course, some people want to hurt us because they themselves are hurting. Asking in this way makes them more accountable for what is coming out of their mouths. This is a way of standing up for yourself without being confrontational. Many times people will walk away thinking, "I should have said this and this." Or, "I am just not good at comebacks to insults until after the fact." Well now you just need to remember the above two questions.

3. Agree with the critic

I suggest using this only if you have healthy self-esteem and won't store the comment in your filing cabinet.

You agree with the critic for one of two reasons.

a) It is true and it is not important enough for you to change.

Ex: "You are a terrible cook."

"Yes, I've heard that before. That is why you should always eat before coming to my house for dinner."

b) It is not true, but when you agree with the person, there is no reason to continue the dialogue and it stops the critic.

"This place is a mess."

"Yes it is."

"Aren't you going to do something about it?"

"Well I haven't so far, so I guess I won't now."

4. Write it down/throw it away

Now you could write it down while they are critiquing you.

"Could you say that again? I want to make sure I got it right."

They ask, "Why are you writing it down?"

Response, "I want to show it to my therapist." ☺

However, this is very confrontational which is not always appropriate.

After you have heard the criticism and you are alone, I suggest writing it down. Check the validity and emotional climate to see if it is attacking or descriptive. If it is criticism that could help you grow and improve, use it. If it is attacking and hurtful, rip it up and throw it away. This makes it more concrete so you don't automatically store it in your "filing" cabinet.

5. Ask for detailed feedback.

Specifically, what would you like changed in this report?"

"If you were in my shoes what would you have done differently?"

"Your perception of the problem is not clear to me. Could you give me some examples?"

The whole point here is to stand up for yourself without being defensive or hostile. Don't just let others dump garbage on you and walk away.

Until we are all that we wish to be, how can we be upset with someone who is not what we wish them to be?

WHAT DO YOU WANT THE END RESULT OF CRITICISM TO BE?

- TO HURT
- TO CHANGE BEHAVIOR

EFFECTIVE FEEDBACK

- DESCRIBE WHAT YOU SEE
- DESCRIBE WHAT YOU FEEL
- DESCRIBE WHAT NEEDS TO BE DONE
- DO NOT ATTACK THE PERSON

7

☺ ☺ ☺

SHRINKIN' STINKIN' THINKIN'

I've learned that our background and circumstances may have influenced who we are but we are responsible for who we become.

In this chapter I want to give you and your children **"A check up from the neck up"** a phrase coined by author Zig Ziglar.

The first step in helping you or your child to change the negative files is changing the negative programs in your own computer. It requires taking control of our self-talk.

Self-talk is the constant talking that goes on in your head. Even right now while you are reading this you may be thinking, "I don't talk to myself, do I?"

Seventy-seven percent of all self-talk is negative. We have thoughts such as:

- Oh, I can tell it's going to be another one of those days.

- Nothing ever goes right for me.

- I'm so clumsy.

- Everything I eat goes right to my waist.

- I can't seem to get organized.

- Today just is not my day.

- With my luck I don't have a chance.

- I'd like to stop smoking but I just can't.

- I don't really have the energy that I used to.

- I'm really out of shape.

- I lose weight but then I gain it right back again.

- I'm so depressed.

Children have thoughts such as:

- Why should I try, it's not going to work anyway.

- I never get a break.

- This class is boring.

- I hate doing math.

- I wish I was never born.

- I hate my hair.

- I don't do well on tests.

- I'll never graduate.

- No one likes to play with me.

- If only I was thinner.

- I'll never be as good as Tom in basketball.

Zig Ziglar calls negative self-talk "Stinkin' Thinkin'" (My high school students referred to it as "verbal vomit").

PUTTING YOURSELF DOWN

- ◆ NEGATIVE SELF-TALK
- ◆ STINKIN' THINKIN'
- ◆ VERBAL VOMIT

Stinkin' thinkin' is self-criticism, which does more damage to your own self-esteem than anyone else can do and it rips many more pieces out of your IALAC sign.

Everyone has a critical inner voice. Your critical inner voice keeps mental pictures of your failures in order to protect you from possible rejection or disappointment in the future. It never keeps track of your successes, only of how you've messed things up.

Let's say you are going to a job interview and you're nervous. Your inner voice automatically kicks in to prepare you for disappointment, so your stinkin' thinkin' may sound like this:

Why am I putting myself through this?

I'm not going to get the job anyway.

There are so many more qualified people.

I never do well in interviews.

This is a waste of my time.

I'll do it for the practice but I know I don't have a chance of getting the position.

Now when the company calls to tell you that you didn't get the job, you can say to yourself, "See I was right. I knew I wouldn't get it."

OR

Let's say you just finished wallpapering a room and a friend comes over to see it. Before they can even compliment you on how nice it turned out, you quickly point out any flaws, flaws so minor they might not have even noticed had you not pointed them out.

Why? Because your critical voice is attempting to protect you by convincing you that it won't hurt as much if you point out the mistake before they see it. "You can't reject my work because I rejected it first."

How many times have you started a project and not finished it? You remodel an entire room and never get around to putting the molding up. Why? An unfinished project cannot be subjected to criticism simply because it is not finished.

If someone criticized the work in the remodeled room you can respond, "Yes, but when the molding goes up it will all tie together." Children do the same thing when they do homework and don't turn it in or when they start building a model airplane and never finish it.

Everyday you and your children dump garbage on yourselves with stinkin' thinkin'. It is important to stop "dumping" this toxic waste on yourselves. We predict failure or success with our words, then we live up to it.

According to Dr. Julie White, the author of *The Psychology of Self Esteem* we have two types of inner voices, a negative and a positive voice.

Dr. White calls them "Mister Rogers" and "Rambo":

1. Mister Rogers is the positive voice that encourages you.

- It is ok, just try again.
- I can do it.
- Keep on trying.
- Don't give up.

2. Rambo is your negative voice.

- I'm such a stupid jerk.
- I'm always making mistakes.
- I'm never going to get it right.
- How dumb can I be?

The voice you listen to will determine how you feel and how you behave. Here is how it works. You have a thought.....the thought determines how you feel.....the feeling determines how you act.

Your child gets dressed up for picture taking day in school

and looks in the mirror...

Thought - I look good.

Feeling - happy, pretty, handsome

Behavior – positive, smile, has a great day in school

Your child has homework...

Thought - I hate homework. It will take me all night.

Feeling - tired, overwhelmed, sick

Behavior - takes a nap, complains, takes all night to do the homework or doesn't do it at all.

After receiving a call from a friend to go bike riding, the same tired, overwhelmed child suddenly feels great, full of energy and ready to go outside. Why? Because his thought process changed from negative to positive.

This backs up the statistic that says 75% of all illness is self-induced through stinkin' thinkin'. Think about this for a moment. When it's time to pay taxes or the in-laws are coming over for a weekend, do you suddenly feel the flu coming on? When you feel you need a day off and want to call in sick so you can go golfing or shopping do you actually start feeling sick before you make the call? "You know...I am starting to get a sore throat".

Stinkin' thinkin' affects our energy and strength.

Here is an activity that I do in my workshops with both adults and students to show how much power your thoughts have over your energy and strength. You may want to try this at home.

In my workshops I use the following demonstration to show how stinkin' thinkin' affects your strength and energy.

1. I ask for a volunteer to come up to the front of the room. I explain we are going to be working with "muscle testing" to see how strong you are and to see how certain thoughts and words affect your strength. I ask the volunteer to extend his right arm straight out at shoulder level, parallel to the floor.

2. I place my hands on the upper part of the volunteer's arm, one near the wrist and one near the elbow. I then press down on the volunteer's arm and say, "I want you to resist my downward motion. Ready? Resist."

3. Push slowly, increasing the pressure in attempt to push the arm down. Usually I'm not able to push the arm very far down. This is called your 'base strength.' We'll be using this base strength measurement to compare all our other tests.

4. I ask the volunteer to lower his arm. I instruct him to repeat a statement out loud with great force and conviction, ten times. The statement is, "I'm stupid and no good."

5. After he has said, "I am stupid and no good" ten times, I ask him to raise his arm again. I push down on his arm again saying, "Ready? Resist."

In most cases, the arm will be dramatically weaker than during the base strength test, and the volunteer will be unable to resist my downward pressure. The arm will easily be pushed down to their side.

There's a second step to this exercise.

6. This time I ask the volunteer to say ten times out loud with the same great force and conviction, "I'm smart and I'm wonderful." Then I ask him to raise his arm.

7. Once again, I apply increasing pressure to his arm saying, "Ready? Resist."

In most of the cases, the volunteer's strength will be as strong as it was at the beginning of the test, if not stronger. I am not able to push the arm down at all.

What this demonstrates is the power of our thoughts over our bodies. When we say negative things to ourselves or to others about ourselves, we tend to weaken our bodies. When we think or say positive thoughts to ourselves, we tend to feel stronger. No one knows why this is true – just that it is. It  makes sense, then, to notice our internal dialogue and begin to say only positive things to ourselves about ourselves.

We can take this a step further and demonstrate how this works in terms of the pictures we imagine in our minds.

1. I have the volunteer close his eyes and think of a time in the past when he had a 'failure experience', a time when he set a goal or tried to do something that didn't work out - a time when he felt he failed to achieve his chosen goal. He will not be sharing this aloud, so he can be as honest as possible. As soon as he has such an event imagined vividly in his head so he can feel, hear, and see what it was like, he lets me know.

2. Now I have the volunteer raise his arm to shoulder level and attempt to resist my pressure. He is usually weak and the arm goes down.

3. Repeat this with a positive, successful experience and the arm will resist the pressure and stay raised.

It's not only the thoughts we think, but also the images and the memories we choose to focus on in our mind, that either weaken or strengthen us. The secret to having any lie believed is merely to repeat it often enough. That is what we do with stinkin' thinkin'!

We don't realize how easily our mind is programmed.

In my workshops I'll ask a person to say 'tin' 10 times fast, and then I ask, "What are aluminum cans made of?" The person almost always says, "Tin". Even though aluminum cans are made of aluminum and they know that, I just programmed them to believe differently.

The human brain will do anything you tell it to do if you say it to yourself often and passionately enough.

Repetition is a convincing argument. You will become what you think about most. Your success or failure in anything depends on your programming. It is a simple but powerful fact. The brain simply believes what you tell it most.

Because this is such an important concept I will explain it in yet another way.

E + R = 0

EVENT + RESPONSE = OUTCOME

We have no control over the events that happen in our lives. How we choose to respond to the events determines the outcome of the event. We have no control over someone not wanting to be our friend, our parents getting divorced, a fire in our house, the weather, somebody cutting in front of us, the teacher or boss we will get, etc. We do have control over how we choose to react to any situation.

Let's say a teenager tries out to be a high jumper on the track team (the event). Each time she attempts to jump over the bar she hits the bar with her foot. If her response is, "Oh I'll never be able to do it this, it's too hard, and this is impossible, why even bother?" The outcome is that she will continue to hit the bar and most likely give up.

If we take the same event but change the child's response, "Next time I'll take a smaller step. Next time I'll lean forward more. I am getting closer. I can do this."

The outcome at the very least will be that they will keep trying and may eventually have success.

To illustrate this concept for adults I will use an example from author Tom Miller.

Event - your spouse brings you flowers

Response - s/he loves me, she cares about me

Outcome - you're very happy you smile, kiss, and hug. It's a pleasant evening.

Now are people always happy when they get flowers? NO!

Event - spouse brings you flowers

Response - suspicious what is s/he up to

Outcome - you throw the flowers, yell, and accuse. It's not a pleasant evening.

Did it have anything to do with the event of getting flowers? NO. It had everything to do with your response to the event.

Let's take it a step further.

Event - spouse brings you flowers because s/he loves you.

Response - s/he loves and cares about me

Outcome - you're happy and s/he gets lucky ☺

Event – your spouse brings flowers because s/he loves you

Response – you think it is because s/he is cheating

Outcome - you're angry and unhappy

We may not choose what happens to us, but we are 100% responsible for how we respond to it.

When you blame others you give up your power to change.

SUCCESS OR FAILURE – IT'S UP TO YOU

- Colonel Sanders, famous for Kentucky Fried Chicken, made 1009 attempts to sell his chicken before he had success.

- Walt Disney had people laugh at his ideas. He was fired for lack of ideas by a newspaper editor. He went bankrupt. Yet he went on to have much success.

- Wilma Rudolph's legs were in braces and was told she would never walk before she went on to become an Olympic track star

- Richard Hooker spent 7 years writing humorous war novels only to be rejected 21 times before they were put on TV and known as "M*A*S*H."

- Flip Wilson was one of twenty- four children. His mom left when he was five years old. His dad was an alcoholic. He ran away eight times by the age of seven and was sent to reform school. He became a successful comedian.

- Babe Ruth had 1330 strike-outs before he set the record for 714 homeruns.

- John Creasy, an English novelist, received 753 rejections notices before he published 564 books.

- Lucille Ball was kicked out of acting school. She wasn't a TV success until the age of forty.

- The editor of Vogue Magazine was told she was not good enough to work for the college paper at Princeton.

These people were 100% responsible for how they responded to events in their lives. They didn't like the results and they were determined not to give up until they reached the outcome they wanted.

If your child runs for class president, what is the worst that could happen? He isn't elected and won't be the class president. He is not class president now, so nothing has changed, yet his stinkin' thinkin' makes him feel like a failure. Each time an action is taken, a result is produced. If it is not the result that is wanted or intended, learn from it, change it, and produce another result.

Your mind can only hold one thought at a time—be it positive or negative.

THE CHOICE IS YOURS.

HOW TO STOP YOUR INNER CRITICAL VOICE

STOP STINKIN' THINKIN'

The first step to changing any behavior is to be aware that it exists. One way to do this, especially for young children, is to put them on a mental diet.

- **Mental diet**

Count your negative self-talk as calories. Put this chart

MENTAL DIET - COUNTING CALORIES

Mom	10	10	10
Sue	10		
John			
Mary	10	10	
Dad			
Grandpa	10	10	10
Our goal is Zero calories at the end of the day!			

on your refrigerator with every family member's name written on it.

Tell the kids, "We're going on a mental diet. Every time you have a stinkin' thinkin' thought or comment, you gain 10 calories. Your goal at the end of the day is to have 0 calories. If you have no calories, you were a positive thinker and you will receive a positive pencil." Positive pencils say things such as:

- I'm going to be somebody

- I'm unique and special

- I can if I think I can

(Those of you who have school-aged children know that when your children sit down to do their homework, they often stare at their pencil. So why not stare at something positive instead of the #2 all of the time? ☺

Children are allowed to catch the adults and give them 10 calories for any negative thought. They will catch others more than themselves, which is OK, because it helps to make them become more aware of what stinkin' thinkin' is, and how often it occurs without realizing it.

You can get rid of those calories by beginning to think positive. If a child say's, "I can't", they get ten calories but if they counteract it by saying "I can. I can. I will." You cross off the ten calories. "I hate cleaning my room. It's too much work" = 10 calories. "I'm capable of cleaning. I can do this if I try." = 10 calories deleted. A child may have 50 calories at the end of the evening and begin to run around saying, "I can, I can, I will, I am lovable and capable". Of course, you know they are doing this so you will delete the calories and they will get their reward and that's OK. The idea is awareness and what new behavior you are looking for to replace the old.

POWERLESS WORDS

• How many times do you and your child use the word "can't".

• How many times do we limit children with the word can't.

"You can't do that."

I had my niece over for the weekend. I asked her to put her shoes on. She made a feeble attempt then said, "I can't do it. I can't do it." To which I replied, We say, "I can. I can. I will." and then we try. By the end of the visit she was saying, "I can. I can. I will" to everything. Two days after she went home, my sister-in-law called me to say, "I am never sending my daughter to your house again." "Why?" I asked, "What did I do?" She replied "Every time I tell her she can't do something she says "I can. I can. I will." (How children manipulate things to meet their needs! ☺ I asked my sister-in-law, "Why do you tell her she can't?" She responded, "Oh, don't give me that positive thinking stuff! If she wants to run out in the middle of the road, what am I supposed to do? Say, 'you can, you can, you will'? I'm not going to let her run out in the middle of the road." I explained, "Can't means not capable. She is capable of running out in the middle of the road but she is not allowed or not permitted." Not being allowed or permitted is different.

In my classroom we are not allowed to use that word "can't" at all. It is like a swear word. If you do, you have to say, "I can. I can. I will" five times to counteract the one negative statement you just put into your computer. One day the school psychologist walked into my room and said, "Listen MaryAnn, I can't make that meeting after school."   My whole class yelled "Oh!!! He used the 'C' word!"

This is the kind of awareness I want. I want them to realize how many times they are stopping themselves with their words because their words are predicting how successful they are going to be in the future. The psychologist could have made the meeting, but a more pressing issue was at hand which took precedence so he chose to forego the meeting. It was a choice.

Can't is a powerless word. You can but you choose not to.

I often say, "I can't cook." (Presently my culinary skills leave much to be desired ☺) However, if it was important to me, if I was willing to put in the time and effort, I could learn to cook, but I choose not to. If you tell yourself you can't, you won't. If you tell yourself you can and make the attempt, you may succeed.

Another powerless word children and adults use is "try"

"I will try to get my homework done."

"I will try to make your party."

"Can you just try to be good for today"?

As Yoda said to Luke Sky Walker in Stars Wars, "There is no such thing as try. You either do or do not"

When you say try to a child, you are saying I expect you to make an attempt but I don't expect success.

Your mind is like a garden; if you don't deliberately plant flowers, weeds will automatically grow. Like weeds, stinkin' thinkin' does not need encouragement. It will automatically grow unless you purposely take the time to plant positive thoughts.

Once you are aware of the words coming out of your mouth, the next step is to change the thoughts, by planting positive thoughts. One way to do this is by using self-talk tapes. Self- talk tapes are audiotapes that repeat positive affirmations over and over. Self-talk tapes deliberately plant positive thoughts. You can buy or make your own tapes. Play the tape as often as possible, even if only as background sound. Play them when your children get up in the morning, when they get dressed, eat, sleep, play video games, when you drive them to school, or while they are doing homework. The positive affirmation will go into the subconscious mind. The more they hear positive statements the more automatic the positive thought becomes.

Pick an area that you or your child wants to improve:

- Self-esteem

- Confidence

- Becoming a better listener

- Fitness

- Organization

- Schoolwork

- Attitude

Now make a tape, listen to it frequently and see what happens.

Have you ever had this experience?

While you are in the supermarket there is music playing in the background that you are not consciously aware of. Later, driving home you find yourself singing a song wondering how that tune got stuck in your head. Self- talk tapes work in a similar way. They are planting positive thoughts in your subconscious mind.

Examples of "self-talk" tapes:

To be a better student:

I enjoy learning. I'm confident in my ability to learn quickly and recall what I learn. I have a sharp, quick and alert mind. I am a good student. I like myself. I enjoy studying. I have an excellent memory and can recall easily what I've learned. I do well on tests. I easily remember what I need to. I earn good grades. I am confident. I feel good about myself. I am relaxed and calm when studying and taking tests. I enjoy learning and remembering what I learned.

To build self-esteem:

I am very special. I like who I am and I feel good about myself. I always work to improve myself and I get better every day. I like who I am today. I have many wonderful qualities. I have talents and skills and abilities. I am discovering new talents inside myself all the time. I am positive. I am confident. I like life and I'm glad to be alive. I have a lot of energy, enthusiasm and vitality. I am glad to be me. I am happy. I smile a lot. I like who I am. I believe in myself.

I used self-talk tapes with one of my special education classes. While they were coming into the classroom in the morning the positive tapes would be playing. Then I would have them put their heads down and consciously listen for 3 minutes. Boy did they complain! However, I continued to play the tapes in spite of their complaints. There was a 12-year-old boy in my classroom named Paul. Every day he would say, "Oh, we have to listen to these boring tapes. I hate these stupid tapes." He moved away from the area for a few months. When he returned to our district and had a choice of returning to my class or going to another, he said to his mother "I want to go back to Mrs. B's class because at least she starts her day with those stupid positive tapes." ☺ Who would have known?

Because I believe in trying things before I speak about them, I made my own self-talk tape in order to eat healthier foods and to lose weight. What you state on a tape is what you want to become true, not what is true. I have a tendency to consume chocolate frequently and in large quantities. It is rare that I eat any fruits or vegetables.

However the tape stated:

"I eat healthy foods. I enjoy eating fresh fruits and vegetables. I weigh a slim, trim 120 pounds."

All of the above are lies. But they state what I would like to be true. I would listen to this tape in the morning when driving, when cleaning, in the evening, and while sleeping. After two weeks of listening to this tape, I went into the refrigerator to get some chocolate pudding. In my hand was a peach. At first I was stunned then recalled, "Oh, that's right, I eat fruits and vegetables." I started to lose weight listening to tapes so guess what I did? I stopped listening to the tape and not long after I went back to my old habits. This does not mean that we have to listen to mind tapes everyday for the rest of our lives. However, it is not possible to reprogram thirty-five years of negative thoughts in just a few weeks. Start off listening to the tapes a few times a day, to once a day, to two times a week and then twice a month to keep the thoughts fresh and positive. It is interesting how we are willing to brush our teeth or shower daily to stay clean. Yet we don't see the value or are not willing to put the effort into practicing daily self-talk to stay positive in such a negative world.

The most difficult thing to do is to play a positive tape when you're depressed or in a negative frame of mind. One solution I found was to purchase a radio/alarm clock that also has a tape player. Instead of having the alarm go off, let the tape play. I would wake up hearing positive comments. The amazing thing about self-talk tapes is how simple and easy it is to reprogram your computer, thereby reprogramming your life to be more positive.

Why will very few people use this simple procedure? Perhaps:

- We are happy being miserable

- We fear change

- We fear success

- It sounds too simple so it must not work

If you are committed to it, it will work. If you want change take action and make it happen. You have nothing to lose and everything to gain.

Model positive self-talk for your children:

Children imitate their parents. Therefore, if you do your positive thinking aloud, then you are modeling for them. You are showing them your thought processes. Instead of hearing, "I can't handle the pressure," they will hear, "I'll take one day at a time until I get through this busy time at work."

Modeling self-talk also teaches kids how to solve problems:

"I am frustrated that this glue stick isn't working. I feel like screaming but that won't make it work so I guess I will ask someone if they will share their glue with me."

"I am so angry right now that I need time to myself to calm down before I talk to you."

GUIDELINES FOR USING POSITIVE SELF-TALK (by Denis Waitley)

1. Use personal pronouns. Words such as 'I', 'my', 'mine', and 'me' will personalize your self-talk and will help you internalize it.

Ineffective Self-Talk	Effective Self-Talk
"People are fun to be around."	"I enjoy being around people."

2. Keep your positive self-talk in the present tense. Referring to the past or future dilutes the impact of your self-talk.

Ineffective Self-Talk	Effective Self-Talk
"Someday I'll get good grades."	"I am doing well in school."

3. Direct your positive self-talk toward what you desire, not away from what you don't want. You want to focus your current dominant thought on your desires, not your dislikes.

Ineffective Self-Talk	Effective Self-Talk
"I can quit smoking.	"I am in control of my habits."
"I will lose 20 pounds."	"I weigh a slim, trim 125 pounds."

4. Keep your self-talk non-competitive, rather than comparing yourself with others.

Ineffective Self-Talk	Effective Self-Talk
"I'll never become a starter on the team"	"I am starting on the team before he or she does."

SELF-TALK

Positive self-talk leads you forward to where you want to go. Negative self-talk locks your door to success.

1. Practice turning the following statements into positive self-talk that reflects the desired results rather than the negative fears.

140

NEGATIVE (FEAR) SELF-TALK	POSITIVE (DESIRE) SELF-TALK
"I'm no good at this."	"I am capable of doing the task."
"I don't feel good."	"I am getting better and better every minute."
"I have to..."	"I choose to..."
"It is too difficult."	"It is a challenge."
"If only."	"Next time."
"I'm afraid."	"I am calm and relaxed."
"I wish..."	"I will."

Now try some on your own

"I'll never make it."

"I can't help it."

"There's too much to do."

"I don't think it'll work."

Positive self-talk doesn't mean you make excuses for yourself when you do something wrong. It doesn't mean you don't have to correct your mistakes. It means that instead of getting down on yourself, you coach yourself into doing what you are supposed to do.

Positive self-talk is not bragging. It is reminding yourself (not others) about something that is true and good about you. You are encouraging yourself like a good friend would.

This poem summarizes what we have been discussing in this chapter

Today

Outside my window, a new day I see,
And only I can determine what kind of day it will be.
It can be busy and sunny, laughing and gay,
Or boring and cold, unhappy and grey.
My own state of mind is the determining key,
For I am only the person I let myself be.
I can be thoughtful and do all I can to help,
Or be selfish and think just of myself.
I can enjoy what I do and make it seem fun,
Or gripe and complain and make it hard on someone.
I can be patient with those who may not understand
Or belittle and hurt them as much as I can.
But I have faith in myself, and believe what I say
And I personally intend to make the best of each day
                          By Jan Lavalley

Positive thinking will not let you do anything: but it will let you do everything better than negative thinking will.

8

☺ ☺ ☺

HEAR THE REAL MESSAGE BEHIND THE WORDS

"Those who think they know it all
have no way of finding out they don't"
Leo Buscaglia

"We were given two ears but only one mouth,
because listening is twice as hard as talking "
Larry Nadig

People are in institutions because no one
would listen to their stories.
Carl Jung

Communication skills are the most important skills we need in life. Without them we are doomed to continual frustration and misunderstandings. How often have we said or heard this comment: "Talking to you is like talking to a wall."

Communication skills are your family inheritance. You may not be able to leave your children a large fortune, but here is one legacy that all parents leave their children whether they want to or not - the family communication strategies.

In northern Thailand where there was no electricity or telephone service, the family built a fire outside the home and sat around talking with each other for two hours every evening. Everyone in that culture learned to tell stories and to listen. In our culture few people are taught to listen.

Very few children know how to express feelings or listen to others' feelings. Children who grew up under the "Kids should be seen and not heard" theory were deprived of the opportunity to express their thoughts and opinions and to gain confidence in their own abilities.

Children and adults feel rejected, angry, unimportant, worthless, and unloved when they are not heard. Therapists rely on listening, not talking, and for good reasons. People need to vent their feelings so they can dissipate the pressures building inside. Unless she listens, a therapist cannot possibly know what her patient's problems are. What works for a therapist in a clinical setting can work for you at home. Expressing our wants, feelings, thoughts and opinions clearly and effectively is only half of the communication process. The other half is listening and understanding what others communicate to us. That is what our focus will be in this chapter.

There is a real distinction between merely **hearing the words** and **listening for the message**. When we listen effectively we understand what the person is thinking and/or feeling from the other person's own perspective; It is as if we were standing in the other person's shoes, seeing through his/her eyes and listening through the person's ears. Our own viewpoint may be different and we may not necessarily agree with the person, but as we listen, we understand the other's perspective. To listen effectively, we must be actively involved in the communication process and not just listening passively. We all act and respond on the basis of our understanding, and too often there is a misunderstanding that neither party is aware of. With active listening, if a misunderstanding has occurred, it will be known immediately, and the communication can be clarified before any further misunderstanding occurs.

Adults usually react to children's statements in one of two ways: either approval or disapproval. Yet, the most helpful response for children is often nonjudgmental, responding in a way which identifies feelings, recognizes wishes, and acknowledges opinions. Authors Faber and Mazlish teach ten ways to communicate effectively with your child.

144

1. Use eye contact and listening body language

Avoid looking at your watch, at other people or activities around the room. Face and lean toward the speaker and nod your head. Be careful about crossing your arms and appearing closed or critical. Use facial expressions (smile, frown, shock) to reflect a child's feelings and nod to show you are listening. Non- verbal listening techniques show you are interested. Eye contact is critical to listening. Stop and look at your child to show you are listening and are interested.

I was shopping in a clothing store and a little girl was with her grandmother. The grandmother was looking at the dresses and the girl was saying "Oh, grandma! The baby chick hatched and it was so tiny. It was this tiny and it was so cute." The grandmother was saying all the right things, "Oh, that must have been exciting. It must have been such fun to watch that chick come out. Oh, wow! I can't believe it was that tiny." The little girl said "But grandma, how do you know? You didn't turn around and look." The little girl was using her finger to show how tiny it was. Eye contact does make a difference.

Think about how you give hints to people in your office or classroom that you need to leave and don't want to listen anymore. You pack up your desk, look at the clock, or move towards the door. Your body language is saying "not interested - got to go". In a similar fashion with your children, you are so busy running around the house while your child is telling a story you give them the message they are not important enough for you to stop and listen.

I was in a store one day and a little boy was attempting to tell his dad about how far he kicked his ball in a kickball game. The father was distracted looking for something. He was looking around the store and the little boy was saying in a very excited tone, " I kicked the ball so far! Everybody ran. I got home and it was so great!" The father responded with, "Oh really, uh huh."

145

Little boy, "Daddy! Did you hear me? I kicked the ball across the field. It was so far."

The father, "Uh huh, uh huh."

The boy, "Daddy, you know how far I kicked that ball?"

The father, "Enough already, I heard you kicked the ball, now shut up."

The father was getting angry because he heard this story three times. However the young boy was repeating it over and over. Why? Because he didn't feel he was heard or acknowledged the first three times. The father could have acknowledged the son's feelings simply by taking a moment to look at him and say, "Wow, that is exciting! It sounds like you are very proud of how far that ball went."

2. Allow, acknowledge and validate the feelings

All feeling are permitted, actions are limited.

We must not deny a child's perceptions. This does not mean you are giving in to them nor does it mean you agree with them. It means you understand the feeling. Be empathic and nonjudgmental. You can be accepting and respectful of the person and their feelings and beliefs without giving up your own position, or without agreeing to the accuracy of their view.

By feeling the child's emotion, it tells the child that all feelings are important, both the good and the bad. Once your child's angry and hurt feelings are out in the open, heard and accepted, he can change them. Sometimes children just need to be heard and acknowledged before they are willing to consider an alternative position.

We deny hurt feelings because we don't want people we care about to be unhappy. In an attempt to make them feel better, we tend to minimize or deny their feelings. This doesn't make them feel better, it makes us feel better. It's OK to have negative feelings. You do not have to make them feel better. Actually, just listening and accepting the feeling helps a person to feel better.

A common communication mistake is to deny the feeling or minimize it:

"Oh stop your crying, you fell on the rug; it couldn't have hurt that much"

"It is not a big deal, not everyone makes friends on the first day of school."

Imagine you telling a friend, "Oh I am so nervous about starting my new job"?

They say, "What is there to be nervous about. Don't be foolish. You have no reason to be so worried. You are making a big fuss over nothing." Does this help you relax? NO! It makes you feel inadequate and wrong for having such feelings. What your friend is unconsciously saying is your feelings are stupid; they are ridiculous and should not be trusted.

We do the same things to children.

- "How could you be tired; you just took a nap?"

- "You can't be hungry; you just ate lunch?"

- "How could you feel hot; it is cool in here?"

- "Your finger can't hurt? It's just a little scratch."

When you say this to a child, they cry harder and louder to prove to you that the scratch does hurt. "I see you have a scratch; sometimes small scratches can hurt more than deep cuts" is a response that lets them know they were heard and understood.

Minimizing teaches children not to trust their own feelings, not to listen to their inner voice. Certainly parents don't mean to hurt children with the above responses, they think they are helping; however, they are telling children over and over again:

- You don't mean what you say

- You don't know what you know

- You don't feel what you feel

A child is gifted at playing the piano, yet before each performance she cries and complains of nervousness to the teacher.

Invalidating responses:

- "You have nothing to worry about."

- "The audience doesn't know if you make a mistake."

- "You're terrific; go and prove it to them."

Validating response:

"It's scary to play in front of all those people. It is natural to feel nervous."

"Take a deep breath and keep reminding yourself that you have practiced and are prepared."

Practice validating feelings:

- "I don't want to go to school."

"The first day of school can be scary. There are so many new things to get used to."

- "Only two more days till my birthday!"

"I can hear how excited you are. You must really be looking forward to that special day."

Your turn:

- "I can't do this project; it is too hard for me."

- "Those stupid teachers wouldn't let us go out for recess because it rained."(Hint: Don't address the word stupid;

that is just their way of letting you know how disappointed they are)

3. Give the feeling a name

"That sounds frustrating"

"I imagine that must have been frightening"

Don't respond to just the meaning of words, look for the feelings or intent beyond them. The surface meaning of words used by children is not the message. Identifying and naming the feeling helps the child to realize that you do understand. It also expands their vocabulary so they can better express themselves in the future. Adults fear they will make it worse by suggesting a feeling, but in fact the child feels comforted because someone has acknowledged their inner experiences. Adults also fear they will guess the wrong feeling. If you get the feeling wrong, that's ok; the child will correct you. This is helpful in decreasing miscommunication.

"I can't believe I have to do this report over again."

"You sound angry that you were asked to rewrite the report".

"No, I am just worried I won't have enough time with all my other work."

4. Match the intensity with vocabulary

The feeling word should match the intensity level.

If a horrible injustice has just been done to you and your friend says," Sounds upsetting" That doesn't even come close to how you are feeling, so you rant and rave even more to show how upset you are. When your friend says, "You must have been outraged!"

You think, "Exactly. Finally someone understands how I feel!"

Examples of different intensity levels of fear from strong to mild are:

Panicked = terrified = scared = worried = anxious = nervous = uncomfortable

Be careful not to over-emphasize emotions.

 "Tommy hit you! You must feel like killing him!" This is going overboard. ☺

5. Listen without interruption

Another common communication mistake is giving advice or trying to solve others' problems rather just listening to feelings.

Have you ever come home angry with your boss and as you are venting to your spouse they bombard you with questions and advice.

"Did you tell him...? Do you think ... why didn't you...? You should have...."

You just want him to be quiet and listen and understand how you feel. You don't necessarily need or want advice. In fact you are so upset you don't even hear the advice. You just need to vent and be validated.

Children often need to vent, yet we stifle the feeling and give solutions:

"I hate Tommy; I wish he was never born."

"Don't say that. He is your brother. I'm sure you don't mean it. Just be more patient with him. He is little, you were little once, remember?"

Instead:

"Sometimes it is hard to share your mom's attention with someone else" or

"Having a new baby in the house can be difficult. It sounds like you're feeling left out. What can we do about that?"

By giving a child immediate advice or giving an instant solution, you deprive them of the experience that comes from wrestling with their own problems and emotions.

I was attending a family party and my brother's little girl came up to him crying,

"Daddy, nobody wants to play with me". Sob....Sob.

He picked her up and I thought he was going to say, "Hey, there are lots of kids here, go find someone else to play with." Instead he said, "I see you're upset and feeling left out." She wiped her tears and said; "Yeah" Then jumped down from his arms and ran to find someone else to play with! What really kills me about this story is. He doesn't even read any of these parenting books, he just did it naturally! ☺

Children don't really need or want us to solve their problems all of the time. They just want us to understand how they feel. If we want to get to the real meaning behind the message we need to listen and not rush to solve their problems. Resist the temptation to make things better.

When a child has a cut, we clean it and put a Band-Aid on it. We know in time it will heal. Wounds of the spirit are the same. The Band-Aid is the validation that helps to start the healing process.

6. Listen without talking about your own experience

Don't make it about you.

When a child or friend is telling a story, happy or sad, and we have had a similar experience, we tend to just jump in and tell our story. We tell how we had a similar situation. We make the story about us. It is not about you.

"Oh yeah I remember when I was in school and the kids would call me names, it would upset me also. I would just try to ignore them, you should do the same."

We don't do this because we are uncaring people. We do it because we care. We want them to know we understand just how they feel. It is our way of empathizing. But at this point they don't care about how you felt. It's a new feeling for them. It is their experience. They can better listen to your story after they have shared and feel their story has been heard. Listen, validate and then ask, "I had a similar situation when I was in school; would you like to hear about it?"

7. Paraphrase

To assure your child that you heard and understood what they are feeling, in your own words interpret what was said. Do not repeat back the exact words. This is called parroting. Parroting back the words verbatim is annoying and does not ensure accurate understanding of the message. When you parrot, not only does it annoy the child it also shuts down communication.

CHILD "I am so mad at dad"

MOM   "So you are mad at dad"

CHILD "Duh, isn't that what I just said?"

CHILD: "I don't like David anymore!"

PARENT: "So you don't like David?' (parroting)

152

PARENT: "Something about David bothers you?

OR

"Sounds as if you are really annoyed with him?"
(paraphrasing)

8. Accept the pain without repeating the name

Don't repeat the names children call themselves

"I am so stupid"

"Oh, so you think you are stupid?"

"I am the ugliest person on earth.

"You feel you are really ugly."

A better choice:

"The teacher said it should only take 15 minutes, it took me an hour. I must be dumb"

"It can be discouraging when work takes longer than you expect."

"My haircut looks awful. I am so ugly."

"It sounds like you are disappointed in the way your hair was styled."

You may be wondering, why can't we just say I understand how you feel? It's simple. They don't believe it! Your words, your facial expression, and your tone of voice let them know you really do understand.

9. Give a student wishes or fantasy

When children want something they can't have, adults usually respond with logical explanations of why they can't have it. The harder we explain the harder they protest. Sometimes just having someone understand how much you want something makes reality easier to bear.

153

EXAMPLES:

If you have no ice cream in the house and your child wants ice cream, instead of saying, "We have none so just deal with it."

TRY:

"I wish we had a freezer full of ice cream for you to eat. However, there are cookies in the cabinet for a snack."

You are on vacation and forgot your child's favorite blanket:

"I can't sleep without my blanket"

"I know you really miss your blanket. I wish I had a magic wand and could make your blanket appear."

It helps to decrease the length of the tantrum!

I was babysitting for my niece who at the time was about two or three years old. She was sick and the doctor said she was not allowed to have milk in her bottle. When it was time to go to bed, she started crying because she wanted a bottle of milk instead of the bottle of the juice I was offering her. I, being the irrational adult, attempted to explain why she could not have the bottle of milk.

"Your tummy is sick. The doctor said milk would make it hurt more."

Do you think she really cared or was even listening? She just continued to cry.

I decided to try giving wishes.

I said, "I wish I could fill your whole crib with hundreds of milk bottles and you could drink as many as you want. Here is a bottle of juice you can drink that won't upset your tummy."

She stopped her crying, looked at me and said, "My whole crib?"

154

It worked! I was so excited!

I love it when you try a new technique and it works!

Will it always work? NO, however, it will usually decrease the length of the temper tantrums because the child knows that you really understand what they want and how they feel, and the more tools you have in your tool belt the better equipped you are to deal with different situations.

Giving wishes works with adults too. Let's imagine you have just lost a loved one and you are beside yourself with grief. I could say, "I wish there was something I could do to take away the pain. I am here if you need me to do anything". It doesn't take away the pain, but you will feel comforted that someone understands and cares.

10. Validate without using the word "BUT"

When you validate and then use the word "but" it negates the validation. It says you don't understand and just want to get in your point:

"I know you're upset that you can't play because it is time for bed, but you need your sleep otherwise you will be cranky in the morning."

"I wish you could play all day, but we have to go to bed."

Instead

"You are having so much fun playing you wish you could do it all night. I'll meet you in your bedroom in two minutes."

Say the same thing without the "but" and you will be amazed how much less resistance you get.

Instead of starting reflective listening statements the same way each time, here are a number of different ways to start:

- It appears

- It seems

- It looks like

- It sounds like

- I notice

- I see that

- If I hear you correctly

- If I understand you correctly

- Could it be

- I'm sensing

- I understand

All of this is easier said than done. Like any skill, it takes practice and in the beginning feels very unnatural. When something does not feel comfortable we tend to think it is wrong and abandon it. When I went to Australia and had to drive on the opposite side of the road and sit on the opposite side of the car, it did not feel natural. Had I done what felt right I would not be here to write this book. When you stick to a new habit for a period of time, it becomes a natural part of your repertoire.

Change is scary. No one likes change except babies in wet diapers. Change takes time. Be patient and do not give up on yourself.

Think of the people you call when you need to vent. They often have the listening skills we mentioned. Even though these skills sound phony in isolation, when you are putting them into practice the sender will feel as though you are listening and do care.

Listen Poem

When I ask you to listen to me
And you start giving advice
You have not done what I asked.

When I ask you to listen to me
And you begin to tell. Me why I shouldn't t feel that way,
You are trampling on my feelings.

When I ask you to listen to me
And you feel you have to do something to solve my problem
You have failed me, strange as that may seem.

Listen! All I asked, was that you listen,
Not talk or do-just hear me.

Advice is cheap: 50 cents will get you both Dear Abby and
Billy Graham in the same newspaper.
And I can do for myself; I'm not helpless.

When you do something for me that I can and need to do
for myself, you contribute to my fear and weakness.

But when you accept as a simple fact that I do feel what I
feel, no matter how irrational,
then I can quit trying to convince you and can get about the
business of understanding what's
Behind this irrational feeling.
And when that is clear, the answers are obvious and I don't
need advice.
Irrational feelings make sense when we understand what's
behind them.

Perhaps that's why prayer works, sometimes for some
people because God is mute, and he doesn't give advice or
try to fix things. "They" just listen and let you work it out
for yourself.

So please listen and just hear me. And if you want to talk,
wait a minute for your turn: and I'll listen to you.

Anonymous

Most of the time we don't communicate,
we just take turns talking.

Take responsibility for your own happiness.
Choose to concentrate on what you have
rather than what you don't have.

If you are miserable about all things
you want but haven't gotm think about
all the things you don't want
and haven't got.

Andrews Matthews

9

☺ ☺ ☺

FAMILY MEETINGS

When it becomes more difficult to suffer than change . . . you will change.

Let's look back at the key ingredients we all need in order to possess healthy self-esteem: Safety, Belonging, Identity, Competence and Power. Let's imagine that safety is a table supported by four legs; Belonging, Identity, Competence and Power. These legs give the table support to withstand weight and perform its job. If you take one leg away, the table will wobble, take two legs away and the table becomes unsteady and fragile, take the third and fourth legs away and the table is no longer able to serve its intended purpose. Children, like tables, need these legs/feelings of support in order to be able to function and be productive. Let's briefly review these feelings:

SAFETY:

Children need to feel safe physically and emotionally. When children feel safe they are better able to concentrate and perform because they are not in constant fear of verbal or physical abuse from peers, family members or other adults.

BELONGING:

This is a feeling of being enjoyed, wanted, loved and accepted unconditionally – a feeling that you belong to someone or something that will care for you and protect you – feeling that you have rights that are respected and opinions which are welcomed and listened to. Joining sports groups, church groups or school clubs gives a sense of belonging. Children often will wear the same clothes and listen to the same music as their friends; they will join gangs or cults just to fit in and belong. Foster children are often missing this leg of support as a result of being moved from home to home, never really knowing where they belong or if they will be wanted.

IDENTITY:

This is a feeling of being someone with special value, an awareness of your own unique qualities. There are two questions that help establish identity:

1. Who am I? This involves heritage, name, nationality, and special relationships.

2. What am I? This involves value judgments—how we see ourselves—the labels we give ourselves.

COMPETENCE:

This is a feeling of self-confidence and worthiness—having self-approval regardless of how or even if others approve of us. I am worthy of others' time and attention. Feeling capable gives us the desire to achieve higher goals.

PURPOSE/POWER:

This is a feeling of self-control. It is the ability to make choices and decisions that affect your life. You have beliefs about yourself, such as "I make my own decisions, I don't conform and follow others, I live up to my own standards, I have the ability to reach my goals".

Purpose does not have to be something you climb to the top of the mountain to discover. You could give your child a simple purpose. "I look forward to coming home after work just to see your smile."

My mother would often tell me the story about how I was born almost 2 weeks late (nowadays they would have induced) with the umbilical cord wrapped around my neck three times. She would say, "You are special. You were meant to be here, you have a special purpose." Even though she never told me what the purpose was, just hearing the story and knowing she believed it made me believe I did have a special purpose.

The best way to build these five feelings in a child is through family meetings. Getting together regularly helps create a feeling of unity. Taking time to listen to one another communicates that you have value and importance. When family members know that their views count, they have a greater feeling of belonging. Meeting regularly provides an opportunity to make plans and decisions as a family, which gives a sense of power.

Large and small corporations, PTA organizations, school districts would not be able to function and succeed without communicating with each other about their work, their problems, their goals or ideas. The family is similar to these organizations in that it is made up of individuals, living in the same home, who have different needs and personalities and who have to work as a team in order to grow and live peacefully. In today's hectic pace, families seldom sit down together, even for a meal. In some families, when everyone does get together, the TV set is often the focus of attention. Opportunities to talk things over, as a family are rare. Some parents make all the decisions in isolation. Involving children and giving them a say in decisions that affect them communicates respect and gives them valuable practice in making decisions.

Like an automobile engine that may appear to run smoothly but suddenly boils over unless properly lubricated, families require proper maintenance checks and minor tune-ups. When family meetings are implemented in a positive supportive way, they serve as the lubricant for a smooth running family.

Discussing family plans and concerns as a group offers many benefits:

It creates a feeling of unity and a sense of belonging

Provides a time to express positive feelings

Models communications skills

Models problem solving skills

Gives children a chance to voice their concerns

Enables children to feel their view is heard and respected

Helps children learn to listen to all sides of an issue

Teaches children that blaming doesn't solve problems

Trains children to take more responsibility in carrying out agreements

Leads children to complain less

Helps children learn it is okay to have different opinions

Gives children the feeling they have been heard

Some difficulties with family meetings are:

Finding time for everyone to meet weekly

Energy/patience to listen to children's ideas

It is easier and faster to make decisions alone

Discussions can get heated/difficult

Formal meetings can feel unnatural

Controlling parents may feel threatened

The advantages far outweigh the disadvantages. Do not underestimate the value of family meetings.

In order to find out what topics need to be discussed put a blank sheet of paper on the refrigerator titled: "FAMILY MEETING AGENDA". As issues arise both parents and children write them down on the paper.

It is my belief that the first meeting should be to explain the purpose of the family meetings and to discuss something light or fun, such as planning a family outing or vacation. This meeting should also be used to explain the positions/jobs:

• Secretary - keeps notes of suggestions and decisions from each meeting.

• Chairperson - makes sure everyone is heard, no one dominates the conversation, no one interrupts and everyone stays on topic.

• Time Keeper – watches the clock to move things along and ends the meeting on time.

I recommend that the parents model the jobs for the first few meetings and then rotate the jobs to other members.

GUIDELINES FOR FAMILY MEETINGS

• All members should be present. Encourage children to at least be present in the room even if they choose not to participate.

• Hold weekly or biweekly meetings at a regularly scheduled time and day.

• Post a note in a highly visible place, stating the day, place and time. (On the frig or mirror in the bathroom)

• Keep meetings 10-30 minutes for younger children, 45 –60 minutes for adolescents. Start and end the meetings on time.

• Rotate chairperson and secretary positions.

• Start with compliments for each other. This starts

your meetings in a positive tone. It forces you to remember things that another has done that you may have been too busy to acknowledge earlier. (Thanks for watching your sister while I went food shopping.) or each person can share something new and good that has happened since the last meeting.

• Discuss problems from the agenda that was posted on the refrigerator all week. You may not have time for all the agenda items. You may need to prioritize the list as part of the meeting. If there are no items on the agenda you may choose to do "Heart Sharing"; see topics for this below.

• Brainstorm solutions for conflicts (write down all ideas given, even the silly or ridiculous ones) Use reflective listening to let family members know they were heard. Ask clarifying questions "Are you saying that...?" "Do you feel...?"

• Evaluate the ideas from the brainstorming sessions. I like this idea because . . . I'm not comfortable with this idea because . . .

• Work for consensus or agree to try one solution for a week, then re-evaluate. If the family is not able to agree because someone is not willing to cooperate or emotions are running high, table the matter until the next meeting.

• Summarize the meeting by reviewing decisions and agreements. Agreements should be signed by everyone and posted.

• End with a family activity or game. It is important to end with a game or some type of fun activity. Play cards, go to the park, or play ball in the yard. It is important that the family learns it is ok to disagree. We can love each other, have fun and still disagree with each others' opinions. The purpose of the meeting is to focus on what can be done, rather than why things are not working.

Parents must keep in mind this is not a time to nag, lecture or threaten. Children need to keep in mind that griping or dwelling on past issues is not productive. When you bring your complaint, state why you have it, and bring a solution.

Of course it could go something like this:

I hate Paul. He is a spoiled brat. He bothers me; I suggest we send him to live somewhere else. ☺

You validate the feeling. "Something about Paul's behavior is bothering you. Tell us exactly what he does that upsets you."

You may even write the suggestion down when brainstorming ideas. "Send Paul to live somewhere else."

When it comes time to evaluate solutions simply say, "This does not work for me, because I love Paul and would miss him. Let's come up with a solution that works for both of us."

Be patient with the effectiveness of this process, it takes time. Often children, especially adolescents, will argue, "Why do we have to have these stupid meetings". I encourage you to stick with it because you are providing them with a life-long skill, not to mention that, in the long run, it will save you time and aggravation. You can spend the time nagging, yelling and complaining or you can spend the time discussing and problem-solving. Author Fred Jones has a saying, "Pay me now or pay me later but either way you are going to pay me"

SAMPLE AGENDA of a family meeting:

7:00 Compliments, thanks, appreciation

  Select Chairperson and secretary

7:05 Read the minutes from the last meeting

  Evaluate progress of agreements made

7:10 Discuss new business from the agenda sheet

7:20 Brainstorm ideas, agree on one solution

7:30 Summarize the discussion and agreements

7:35 Play a family game

"HEART SHARING" DISCUSSION STARTERS FOR FAMILY MEETINGS:

I am happy when...

The best time I had with my family was...

I get really angry when...

If I could run the family I would...

The funniest thing I ever saw was...

One thing I am very good at it is....

I am proud of.....

Today I wish.....

A nice thing that happened to me this week was.....

The best gift I ever got was....

The scariest thing that ever happened to me was......

A nice thing someone did for me was....

A nice thing I did for someone was....

One thing I would like to change about myself is...

If I needed a safe place to go it would be.....

My most special possession is....

When I grow up.....

I felt left out when....

A person I would trust with a secret is....

One thing that happened in the last twenty-four hours that made me feel great was....

TIP:

Don't expect your meetings to be perfect, concentrate on what is going well.

This is a new idea–you may have trouble finding the time to put in place–it may feel uncomfortable or unnatural. However, keep this in mind - because something feels uncomfortable at first, it does not mean it's wrong, it's just new.

---

*Winners are those who do the
uncomfortable things that losers won't do.*

An acorn is capable of becoming a mighty oak, but it will never become a giant redwood - No matter how much you push it. Discover your child's nature and then nurture that nature.

Jim Cathcart

10

☺ ☺ ☺

HOW TO HANDLE TEASING

Sticks and stones may break my bones,
but words will break my heart.

They are tired of hearing it. After a time it gets old and frustrating to constantly hear, "He is calling me a name, he is making fun of me again".

If two children were outside fighting, punching, and had bloody noses, you would go out and break up the fight because they are getting hurt. When your child comes to you and says, "He is teasing me" it is because he is hurting. He wants your help to get someone to stop hurting him.

PHYSICAL SCARS HEAL A LOT FASTER THAN EMOTIONAL SCARS AND SOMETIMES EMOTIONAL SCARS NEVER HEAL.

Here is how one boy described teasing, "It is like someone is tapping a pencil on your shoulder. First, it is a nuisance. But then they keep tapping and it becomes red and sore and a little painful. They keep doing it for so long it opens up like a cut and really hurts. Now when anybody touches the shoulder it hurts right away."

When you ignore a request for help from teasing, children make the assumption you don't care. Ask any child who has been teased on the playground, "Did you tell the teachers?" Their response is typically, "They don't do anything. They don't care".

Many parents have trouble at home with siblings teasing each other. Or a child will come home from school and tell you about a teasing incident that happened to him and the standard response parents often give to the child is, "Ignore it! Just ignore it!" Why do we say this? Because as an adult we know that if the victim ignores the teasing, the teaser will get bored and stop teasing. As adults we know the teaser wants reactions and if the victim doesn't give them one, it will stop, hopefully!

If I walked up to you and shouted, "stupid, retard, lame brain, bozo, moron, jerk!" What would you feel like doing? Let me step back and out of your reach before you answer! Do you feel like ignoring? Probably not; it is awfully difficult to ignore comments such as these, yet we expect our children to ignore them. Children do not want to ignore teasing because they feel they have let the teaser get away with a wrongdoing. They feel they have not stood up for themselves and believe the other person won. This is why they call a name back or throw a punch; because it is the only way they know to stand up for themselves. If we want children to stand up for themselves we need to arm them with strategies to use without having to hurt others physically or emotionally.

As a parent, you probably have encouraged your child to ignore putdowns. The ignoring technique can be very effective, especially when a child holds his head high and gives a nonchalant body posture that implies, "You haven't hurt me with your put-down". With training, practice, and self-confidence, ignoring can become an art. However, many children need a larger repertoire of strategies in order to hold their own in a variety of social-conflict situations.

Children often find that, to save face, they need to say something when they receive a put-down. Therefore, we will be focusing on some assertive verbal responses to put-downs, which do not incite retaliation. The goal is to disarm the antagonizer and deflect aggression. We want to teach children to learn how to respond verbally in an assertive but non-aggressive way, using three types of responses. These responses are playful retorts that have the potential of winning respect and leaving a way open for friendship.

There is no one easy technique that will stop teasing. The ideas I am going to give you will not work unless you practice them often with your child and their siblings in non-stressful situations at home. Eventually they will take it outside the home. In a crisis such as a fire, without practice fire drills, a child will react by hiding under the bed rather than respond by running out of the house. To a child, teasing is also a crisis and they will either react with a fist or respond with a skill. How could you expect them to use a skill against teasing when they have had no practice in techniques that will stop it?

After I teach students about the IALAC sign and Stinkin' Thinkin', I teach them how to deal with teasing. I start by discussing the choice of ignoring. Anyone can call a name back. Even a weakling can do that.

It doesn't take any thought or strength to return fire.

You show tremendous strength if you can ignore and walk away. Only the really strong people can walk away.

People who can ignore and walk away have a huge IALAC sign. It is big and thick like a phone book. It does not rip as easily because they feel secure enough with themselves that they don't need to waste their time and energy getting back at the person.

For example:

If an animal attacks an opossum, the opossum rolls over and plays dead. This results in the attacker leaving the opossum alone, and the opossum wins because he didn't waste his time and energy trying to

fight. Instead he outsmarted the attacker.

Many children don't act like the opossum or listen to adults and ignore the attacker because they feel the need to say something so that the attacker knows it is not OK.

We are all familiar with a remote that controls your TV set. We all fight to have control of the remote, to be in charge of changing the channels. It is fun to have the controls. That is why children all over the world play a game called, "GET THE REMOTE." This is how the game works. We all have a remote inside of us, only it does not have numbers, it has feelings. Other people try to get our remote and push our buttons. It's a lot of fun to get someone else's remote and control him or her just like a remote control car. If someone gets our remote, they are in the driver's seat, driving our emotions. If we want to win the game, we need to keep our remote. The only person that should have your remote, the only person who should be pushing those buttons, is you. We do not want to give someone else that kind of power or control over us. If someone teases you and you yell, hit, swear or tease back, you give him your remote and they win.

Comebacks from Building Self-Esteem in the Classroom by Huggin, Manion, Moen states ways to stand up and say something back to the teaser without ripping their sign and without giving up your remote.

Agree with the put-down

While this response may seem foreign, it doesn't imply that your child really agrees with the attacker or the put-down. It is merely an effective way to surprise the aggressor and allow your child to feel strong and composed. Some of my favorites are:

- Hard to believe, isn't it?
- Cool Huh?
- Nice of you to notice.
- That was supposed to be a secret!
- Wasn't that a great mistake?
- Disgusting, isn't it?
- Amazing, but true!
- That's life!

Give a crazy compliment

Crazy compliments tell put-downers that his or her put-down had little effect, and in fact may not even have been understood as a put-down! Many students enjoy using the following kinds of crazy compliments:

- Nice eyebrows!
- Nice shoelaces!
- Nice elbows!
- I like your tonsils!

Make a joke of it

The use of humor disarms the put-downer and gains your child respect. The following comebacks are favorites of some students:

- Has this been bothering you for long?

- Thanks! I've worked hard, people are finally noticing.

- Next time I must remember to bow!

- Wish you wouldn't worry about me so much.

- Stop-you're breaking my heart!

- Would you put that in writing?

- That's #47 on my list of things to fix.

If you respond back with a negative joke about the attacker, then they still win the game. If you say it in a mean negative tone of voice, they win.

Example:

Child 1 "Hi ugly."

Child 2 "Have you looked in the mirror lately?"

Child 2 lost the game because he put Child 1 down. Instead Child 2 could have said, "Thanks for noticing" or "Thanks for the compliment"

Children can make up their own comebacks as long as they are not hurtful.

Really what you are asking them to do is play opossum. Roll over and outsmart them.

How any of the comebacks are said is critical. It needs to be said in a cool and calm fashion. In the classroom I ask the children, "How many of you watch Nickelodeon? Do you remember the Fonze from the TV show Happy Days?" I go on to explain, "When you are getting teased you need to be cool like the Fonze. Say your comebacks in a calm, cool matter-of-fact voice.

Along with the comebacks, it is equally as important that children check their self- talk. When teased are they in stinkin' thinkin' or positive thinking mode? When someone teases a child and the child "loses it", it is obvious they are engaged in stinkin' thinkin or they would not be getting so upset.

Positive things to say to yourself when you get a put down:

He's just trying to act cool.

She's just trying to impress the other kids.

He only sees me on the outside. He doesn't know what I'm really like.

She is trying to upset me. I'll just ignore it.

I won't give him the satisfaction of getting upset.

She is angry and just taking it out on me.

He can think what he wants. I'm still a cool kid!

If you hear a negative comment over and over again you may believe it. Repetition is a very convincing argument. So it's important to counteract that negative comment with a positive affirmation, a positive belief about yourself. Here is a phrase I have taught children to use.

"No matter what they say I am still a worthwhile person"

You may choose to say the phrase to yourself or aloud to the person. The rule I give my students is, when someone teases you, you must first use this phrase aloud a maximum of three times and then walk away. If the teasing continues, you can tell me and I will help you. The reason for this is so you have a way to help yourself because adults will not always be there to protect you. However, my students weren't willing to try this in the beginning. They would come up and say "Mrs. B. he is making fun of me."

"Did you use the saying?"

"No. That's so stupid."

"Well, I can't help you."

I began this in September and by February I was beginning to wonder, "Why bother? It doesn't seem to be working!" Then one day a teacher who was on playground duty brought one of my students in and said, "He's one of yours, right?"

"Yes."

She said, "I want you to know I was out on the playground and I heard one of the students calling Chris a bunch of names. Knowing Chris' reputation I raced over expecting to break up a fight. However, when I got there all I heard Chris saying was 'No matter what you say I'm a worthwhile person."

Yes!!! They do listen to what I say! There is a purpose to teaching. ☺ I could hardly believe it. To this day I get goose bumps when I think of that. You know what? I would have never known that Chris used the phrase if my colleague hadn't overheard it. It gave Chris a way out of a fight even if only for that one time, and if it was successful, which it was, maybe he'd use it again. Then it dawned on me, Chris is eleven years old; for eleven years he had been used to throwing a punch or calling a name back. Why on earth would I think that in two or three months this saying was going to make him change? Too often when we try something new and it doesn't work instantly we give up. It takes a lot of time and reprogramming before change occurs.

This phrase is for adults as well as for children. When a boss comes up to you and says, "What a lousy job you've done," respond with, "No matter what you say I'm a worthwhile person." Now, if you lose your job don't come looking for me! ☺ OK, it may not always be appropriate to say aloud; however, you do need to say it to yourself. Someone telling you that you have done a terrible job does not mean you are not a worthwhile person. Unfortunately that is what we tell ourselves with our self-talk.

How will you remember to say this to yourself? The same way commercial jingles get you to remember to buy a product. Repetition!

Let's just test your memory and see how well advertisers have done. See if you can complete the following:

- Double your pleasure double your fun...........(Double Mint Gum)

- Just do it................(Nike)

- Good to the last drop.............(Maxwell coffee)

- Like a rock..................(Chevy)

The repetition technique is what I used to get my students to practice the saying "NO MATTER WHAT YOU SAY OR DO I AM STILL A WORTHWHILE PERSON". The class made an audiotape. They could sing on the tape, rap, or rhyme the saying. They would make their own tape and we would play it when they first entered in the morning, or during free time we would have it playing in the background. Children need to hear the saying over and over again to increase the chances of it becoming an automatic thought when in a name calling crisis.

Words are very powerful. A hammer can be used to build or destroy, just as words can be used to help or hurt. When you receive a present you feel special, happy, loved or cared about. Your words should be like presents you give every day; they should make others feel loved and special.

No one can make you feel inferior
without your permission

Eleanor Roosevelt

WHAT MATTERS MOST IS
HOW YOU SEE YOURSELF!

Self-Esteem is
not only respecting
and accepting yourself,
but also respecting
and accepting others.

11

FORGIVENESS

People would rather be "right" than happy

Why should I forgive them?

They should be apologizing to me.

They are the ones who were wrong.

If I forgive them, they will think it was okay.

They don't deserve to be forgiven.

They haven't even said, "I'm sorry;" they don't even want my forgiveness.

We have all been hurt from mistakes by important people in our lives. When we love, we become vulnerable. We open ourselves to disappointment and hurt. Blame and resentment trap us in the past and victimize us in the present. Forgiveness isn't meant to make us forget; it sets us free from the pain that was undeserved. Forgiveness does not excuse behaviors; it means that you decided to deal with the negative feelings, put them behind you, and move on. The person who hurt you probably did so out of his own weakness or shortcomings. You did not deserve it. Now, you can make the decision to let go of the pain and put it behind you.

In order to explain the importance of forgiveness I will use an example from author Sidney Simon. Imagine waking-up each day with a large suitcase filled with pain from your past. You fill this suitcase with grudges, resentment, bitterness and self-pity. You fill the suitcase with every injustice that was ever done to you, with every memory of how others failed you. Then you shut the suitcase and drag it around behind you, sweating and struggling wherever you go.

Think of how it slows you down, how it makes you tired, irritable and how it saps your energy.

Imagine how quickly you could get from place to place, how much more energy you would have and how much freer you would feel if you didn't have to carry around that large suitcase filled with all your old anger.

If you are holding grudges and walking around with unresolved anger, it will take control of your physical health and emotional well-being. It creates stress. You may be experiencing nightmares, headaches, ulcers, backaches, arthritis, high blood pressure, insomnia or heart attacks. On an emotional level you may have a hard time maintaining relationships, become suspicious, start arguments, withdraw and become intolerant. You become a person filled with hatred and bitterness. These negative emotions not only change who you are, they take away your ability to give because you cannot give away what you do not have. If you have turned into a bitter person because of your resent-ment, you pass this on to your children, your spouse and your parents. It means that those who love you don't get all of you because you are spending all your energy holding a grudge. For the sake of your family members and others you care about, you need to seek the desire and courage to forgive.

It's amazing how many people think that not forgiving gives them power. These people are trying to compensate for the powerlessness they felt when they were hurt. The fact is, not forgiving takes time and energy out of your everyday life and therefore gives others power, not you. Let's say you are upset with the horrible things your parents had done to you in the past. Well maybe they did ruin the first half of your life, but by not forgiving, you are giving them the power to ruin the second half. You can avoid this by facing the pain, forgiving them and then moving on.

STILL HOLDING ON TO GRUDGES

Holding a grudge is like driving a car with the emergency brake on. The car will run, but not at its best. It will be under a lot of stress and the longer you drive with the emergency brake the more you'll wear it down until eventually it is completely worn and no longer able to do its job.

Holding a grudge will wear you down and take away your energy and power. You give the power to the people who have hurt you. People put so much time and energy into making sure they hold a grudge, they have no energy to move forward in their own lives. Why cling to pain? Let go.

"Anger, resentment, bitterness, and hatred are the feelings of which emotional prisons are made." Dr. Phil McGraw

Author Dr. Phil refers to people who carry anger, resentment, bitterness and hatred as trash collectors. They are carrying around garbage that was thrown at them many years ago. "I remember back in 1970 when my dad called me a big fat pig." Yeah, so? It is over and done with; stop carting around old garbage. Drop it off at the dump, so you can move on with your life. Blaming others gets you nowhere. However, we like to use it as an excuse for not achieving our potential. "It is my mom's fault that I lack confidence, can't find a good job and am unhappy." Our parents did the best they could with the knowledge and experience they had, with the emotional frame of mind they were in. It doesn't make what they did right, but to continue to blame them for your misery is fruitless.

Forgiveness is not about the other person; it is about you.

- You don't have to have the other person's cooperation

in order to forgive.

- The other person doesn't even have to know.

- They do not have to be sorry.

- They do not have to admit the error of their ways.

Forgiveness is about you, it is not a gift to them, it is a gift to yourself. Forgiveness is powerful. It rescues you from the pain of anger and resentment. We can't change what happened in the past, yet when we feel wronged, we immediately look to blame others and demand justice. We believe justice is done only when we hurt those who have hurt us. "What is the use of demanding an eye for an eye if, having plucked out the other's eye, we still only have one eye?" What satisfaction is there in causing another to suffer if our pain still remains? Forgiveness is not forgetting, not condoning, it is not absolution. Forgiveness is working through the unfinished business, letting go of the pain and moving on for our own sake. You forgive so you can get rid of the excess emotional baggage that has been weighing you down and holding you back.

Sidney Simon, in his book *Forgiveness* puts it simply: "If the person who hurt you offered an apology, would that actually relieve your pain? Could they actually do anything that would compensate for the injuries or injustices you suffered? It would not relieve your pain or take away the resentment. It would not change your life or make you happier, healthier, or more at peace with yourself. You are the only one that can do that. All the years you have waited for them to make it up to you and all the energy you expended trying to make them change or make them pay kept the old wounds from healing. The person may never change. Inner peace is found by changing yourself, not the people who hurt you."

Forgiveness is not "I will forgive you if ... or when...." It is - I will forgive you because I must if I ever hope to continue to love fully and enjoy the present and future. Forgiveness is an action of the will. It is a choice. We either choose to forgive or we do not. If we hope to be forgiven for a wrongdoing, then we must to do the same. If we are unable to forgive others, we cannot expect them to forgive us.

What are your children learning?

When you hold grudges and cut the people out of your life because they have wronged you or they made mistakes, then your child is learning they also could be cut out of your life if they make a mistake. It shows them your love is conditional. This is not the message we want them to learn.

APOLOGIZE

When you make a mistake, or do or say things that are hurtful to family members, it is important to apologize.

I have a friend who told me her mother never once said; "I'm sorry." Now as an adult, she believes that you shouldn't apologize because it will show weakness. It does not show weakness to forgive; it shows you are human and you value your emotional well-being.

What if the same behavior you have forgiven continues to reoccur? Should you keep accepting the apology? People do not change over night. It takes time. The same behavior may occur for a while before it changes. Many parents tell their children, "Don't say I'm sorry. Show me you are sorry by changing your actions." Yes, this would be ideal, but it is not likely to happen over night if you are asking them to change a habit. Have you ever moved the garbage can in your kitchen? For the first few weeks you keep throwing garbage on the floor where the garbage used to be, because it's a habit. It takes time to change old habits, but this does not mean you are not trying.

One mother yelled at her child often. She would tuck her daughter in at night and say, "I'm sorry for yelling. I am working on changing." The daughter's response was, "That's

OK mommy, but you have been working on that for a long time. Can you hurry it up?"

ACCEPTING AN APOLOGY

Many people will accept an apology by saying "OK," or "it's all right". No, it was not all right. Instead we need to say and teach children to say, "I forgive you" Or "I accept your apology". Then let it go and move on.

Leo Buscaglia in the book, *Loving Each Other*, speaks on forgiving each other. He says: "Let's keep in mind that there is nothing wrong with us if forgiveness comes hard. We are simply human, vulnerable and far from perfect. The wrong the people do us is difficult to deal with, especially when we are innocent and can find no explanation for another's behavior. Why should we forgive and forget. We forgive for the price we pay, for not forgiving is too great. To bear grudges, to harbor hate, to seek revenge, are all self-defeating and lead us nowhere. They neither satisfy nor heal. They keep us from moving forward and starting again. They bury positive energies in negative actions, which serve only to exhaust and deplete us. They keep us suspicious and hesitant to trust again. They destroy our creativity and retard our growth."

Forgive yourself

The last and most important thing is to forgive yourself for mistakes you have made with your children or loved ones. You are human. You have and will continue to make mistakes.

AS A PARENT, DON'T BE AFRAID TO ADMIT THAT YOU'VE MADE MISTAKES.

Feeling guilty over mistakes does not help you change; it just keeps you in the victim role and erodes your self-esteem. Guilt also drains you of your energy and love. Forgive yourself for past mistakes. Mistakes are successful if you learn from them. Mistakes indicate success because you were willing to try something new.

There is no such thing as a perfect parent. You do the best you can with the skills and the knowledge you have. Each day you are learning more. You cared enough about yourself and your children to buy this book and read it, in an attempt to improve. If you make a mistake tomorrow, that is OK; the good thing about parenting is you have 365 days for the next 21 years to keep on trying till you get it right. ☺

If you give up on yourself you are giving up on your child. Remember the better you feel about yourself the better you are at all that you do. When you fly on a plane they tell you to first put on your oxygen mask then the child's. They realize that you will be of little help to your child if you don't first ensure that you are taken care of. We need to attend to ourselves in order to be effective in meeting our children's needs.

You can be happy or you can be justified.
You can't be both.

THE WAY YOU WANT IT TO BE

If your path is filled with brambles and thorns
   instead of flowers and trees,
You can be assured it started in your mind
   it's the way you want it to be.

If you're surrounded with turmoil and strife
   not peace and harmony,
You can be assured it started in your mind
   it's the way you want it to be.

If prosperity is only a word
   and you're living in poverty,
You can be assured it started in your mind
   it's the way you want it to be.

When relationships are all out of whack,
   if your love boats are all out to sea,
This, too, you'll find just started in your mind
   it's the way you want it to be.

So start today, use this easy way
   to create a life that's free.
Just close your eyes and visualize
   the way you want it to be.

Betty R. Wilson

12

☺ ☺ ☺

SELF-ESTEEM IN REVIEW

1. Do the IALAC demonstration with your children. This will give you a foundation for future discussions.

2. Use only positive labels and nicknames.

3. Teach children to take charge of their inner computer — filter information given by others.

4. Use a "secret code word" to prevent jokes from going too far and becoming hurtful.

5. Accept children as a unique individual instead of comparing them to others.

6. When a child makes a request, use "ask me later" rather than "maybe".

7. Use a slow, CALM voice instead of yelling. (Pretend to be Bond, James Bond)

8. Love your child without conditions.

9. Show your children affection with a smile, have warmth in your tone of voice, and use a pat on the back, a wink, or a **HUG!**

10. Tell your children "I love you"— They need to hear this often.

11. Give specific/descriptive praise.

12. Give positive attention— focus on the positive rather than the negative.

13. Create a feeling of importance by spending time with your child. Spend quantities of time with your child in order to get those quality moments.

14. Show interest in what your child is doing by attending sports activities, plays and school functions.

15. Never do for kids what they can do for themselves.

16. Write the values down that you want to instill in your children.

17. Write a plan on how to teach and model these values.

18. Remember actions speak louder than words. Be a positive role model.

19. Live in the present moment, stop worrying about the past or future.

20. Use TV PUNCH CARDS to help reduce TV time.

22. Monitor what your child is viewing on TV and on the Internet.

23. Describe instead of criticize. Focus on the behavior you want in the future.

24. Admit your mistakes and apologize. It is okay not to be perfect. **"You can't be perfect and learn at the same time."**

25. Change your Stinkin' Thinkin' to positive thinking.

26. Avoid using powerless words such as "can't" or "try".

27. Make and listen to self-talk tapes.

28. Listen and respect a child's feelings. Validate the feelings without using the word "BUT".

29. Begin family meetings.

30. Keep your remote. Don't let others push your buttons.

31. Practice and frequently review skills with your child on how to handle teasing.

32. Forgive yourself and others.

33. Be patient. Remember it takes time for change to occur.

34. Celebrate what is working.

35. Make time for yourself. Take care of you. The better you feel about yourself the better you can help your children.

VALUING YOURSELF IS THE GREATEST GIFT
YOU CAN GIVE YOUR CHILDREN

CHILDREN ARE KITES

I see children as kites
You spend a lifetime
trying to get them
off the ground.
You run with them
Until you're both breathless...
They crash...
You add a longer tail...
They hit the rooftop
You pluck them out of the spout.
You patch and comfort,
Adjust and teach.
You watch them lifted by the wind and
assure them that
someday they'll fly.
Finally they are airborne,
But they need more string
So you keep letting it out.
With each twist
There is sadness
That goes with the joy,
Because the kite
Becomes more distant,
and somehow you know
It won't be long before
that beautiful creature
will snap the lifeline
That bound you together
And soar as it was meant to soar
Free and alone.

ERMA BOMBECK 5/15/77

SELECTED BIBLIOGRAPHY

Briggs, Dorothy.
Your Child's Self-Esteem.
Dolphin Books, 1975

Buscaglia, Leo.
Living, Loving, Learning.
New York, Ballentine Books, 1982

Canfield, Jack and Harold Wells.
100 ways to enhance self-concept in the classroom.
New Jersey: Prentice-Hall, 1976

Dinkmeyer, Don and Gary McKay.
The Effective Parent.
AGS, 1987

Dyer, Wayne. *The Sky's the Limit.*
New York: Simon and Schuster, 1980

Faber, Adele and Elaine Mazlish.
How To Talk So Kids Will Listen &
How To Listen So Kids Will Talk.
New York: Avon Books, 1999

Helmstetter,Shad.
What To Say When You Talk To Your Kids.
New York: Simon Schuster, 1989

Huggins, Pat and Donna Manion.
Building Self- Esteem in the Classroom.
Colorado: Sopris West, 1994

McGraw, Phillip.
Life Strategies.
New York: 1999

Neslen, Jane.
Positive Discipline.
New York: New York: Ballantine Books, 1996

Samalin, Nancy.
Loving Your Child Is Not Enough.
New York: Penguin Books, 1987

Simon, Sidney and Suzanne Simon.
*Forgiveness. How to Make Peace With Your Past
And Get on With Your Life.*
New York: Warner Books, 1991

Waitley, Denis.
The Winning Generation.
Iowa: Advanced Learning Consultants, 1997

Weisinger, Hendrie.
How To Give Criticism and Get Results.
(Audio Tape) Illinois: Nightingale Conant, 1999

White, Julie.
Self- Esteem For Woman.
(Audio tape) Colorado: Career Track

Young, Bettie.
The 6 Vital Ingredients of Self-Esteem.

Ziglar, Zig.
See You At The Top.
Pelican Publishing Company.2000

INDEX

CHAPTER EIGHT
Communication
- Three common communication mistakes
- How to hear the real meaning behind the message
- Getting children to hear what you are saying

CHAPTER NINE
The purpose of family meetings
The advantages and disadvantages
Guidelines to conducting a family meeting

CHAPTER TEN
Holding on to anger, whom does it really hurt?
Forgiveness, how and why?

CHAPTER ELEVEN
How to handle teasing

CHAPTER TWELVE
Self-Esteem in review

ABOUT THE AUTHOR

MaryAnn has been in the field of education for over 20 years. As a special education teacher she worked with emotionally and learning disabled students from pre-school through high school. She holds an M.S. in Family/Child Counseling, a B.S. in Elementary and Special Education and is an adjunct instructor at Marist College and SUNY New Paltz.

Out of her passion for teaching and love for children she designed and implemented a variety of training programs for educators and parents on self-esteem and discipline.

MaryAnn is available for keynotes, in-service training, student assemblies and parent workshops. For more information or to schedule MaryAnn to speak call, fax, write or email:

MARYANN BRITTINGHAM

1530 INDIAN SPRINGS ROAD

PINE BUSH, NY 12566

Phone: 845-744-3213   Fax: 845-744-3250

E-mail: Mirror38@aol.com

Web page:www.reflectionsseminars.com